RESUME
BUZZ WORDS

GET YOUR RESUME TO THE
TOP OF THE PILE!

Erik Herman
and Sarah Rocha

Adams Media
Avon, Massachusetts

Published by Adams Media, an F+W Publications Company
57 Littlefield Street
Avon, MA 02322
www.adamsmedia.com

ISBN: 1-59337-114-4

Printed in Canada

J I H G F E D C B A

Library of Congress Cataloging-in-Publication Data
Herman, Erik.
Resume buzz words / Erik Herman and Sarah Rocha.
p.   cm.
ISBN 1-59337-114-4
1. Resumés (Employment)--Terminology. 2. Job hunting--Terminology.
I. Rocha, Sarah. II. Title.

HF5383.H46 2004
650.14'2--dc22

2004010018

This publication is designed to provide accurate and authoritative information with regard to the subject matter covered. It is sold with the understanding that the publisher is not engaged in rendering legal, accounting, or other professional advice. If legal advice or other expert assistance is required, the services of a competent professional person should be sought.

—From a *Declaration of Principles* jointly adopted by a Committee of the American Bar Association and a Committee of Publishers and Associations

Many of the designations used by manufacturers and sellers to distinguish their products are claimed as trademarks. Where those designations appear in this book and Adams Media was aware of a trademark claim, the designations have been printed with initial capital letters.

This book is available at quantity discounts for bulk purchases.
For information, please call 1-800-872-5627.

CONTENTS

INTRODUCTION

RESUME BUZZ WORDS is a vital tool for anyone hoping to craft a targeted, effective resume and land his or her dream job. Using the tools and strategies presented here will help you stand out in this very competitive job market. This book is comprised of the following sections.

Part One: Industry Buzz Words

Industry-specific chapters containing buzz words that will make your resume stand out to the hiring managers and human resource professionals reviewing them. Each chapter contains a list of commonly filled positions, a list of buzz words, a list of regularly used action verbs, and example sentences using the buzz words and action verbs in context.

Part Two: Powerful Words for Every Resume

The chapters in this section contain lists of action verbs and adverbs (containing 400 of each) that you can employ to make your resume more varied and effective, no matter what field you are trying to get a job in. In addition, a list of 60 desirable traits will help you decide what to highlight on your resume. Whether you're applying for a job in aerospace, retail, or wholesaling, potential employers will be looking for many of these professional and personal characteristics.

Part Three: A Handbook for Jobseekers

The first chapter in this section covers all the nuts and bolts of putting the buzz words throughout the book into well-crafted and effective resumes and cover letters. Different resume formats will be discussed, as well as what to put on (and what to leave off) your resume. We review the benefits and drawbacks of professional resume writers and the importance of a follow-up letter and thank-you notes.

The final chapter of the book gives you a thorough introduction into the process of conducting a job campaign that will land you the position that's right for you. You'll find sections on job-hunting techniques that work and those that don't; how to develop and approach contacts in your field; how to research a prospective employer; and how to use that information to get an interview. A section on interviewing informs you about interview dress code and etiquette, the "do's and don'ts" of interviewing, preparing for an interview, and more. The chapter concludes by dealing with some of the unique problems faced by those jobseekers who are currently employed, those who have lost a job, and college students conducting their first job search.

For every jobseeker daunted by the long odds of getting noticed in a sea of applicants, *Resume Buzz Words* provides a way to convert your experience and skills into the most powerful resume and job-search campaign possible. It will give you the edge you need to get noticed, get an interview, and get an offer for the job that you really want.

PART ONE

INDUSTRY BUZZ WORDS

CHAPTER ONE

ACCOUNTING AND FINANCE

ACCOUNTING AND FINANCE buzz words highlight experience with accounting, budgeting, treasury, auditing, and information systems activities. This includes collection, documentation, and analysis of financial data and the use of this data to make strategic decisions and share pertinent information with investors, regulators, and government entities. It also includes allocation of capital required for annual operations as well as growth.

COMMON POSITIONS INCLUDE:

Accountant

Accounting Assistant

Accounting Clerk

Accounting Manager

Accounts Payable Clerk

Accounts Receivable
    Clerk

Actuarial Analyst

Administrative Assistant/
    Program Assistant

Administrative Marketing
    Assistant

Assistant Portfolio Manager

Audit Manager

Auditor

Bank Administrator

Bank Treasurer

Benefits Specialist

Billing Clerk

Billing Supervisor

Bookkeeper

Bookkeeping Clerk

Budget Analyst

Business Analyst

Call Center Manager

Certified Public Accountant
(CPA)

Chief Financial Analyst

Client Technology Lead
Developer

Collections Officer

Commercial Loan Specialist

Commercial Operations
Specialist

Credit Analyst

Credit Manager

Director of Research

Equity Research Analyst

Equity Trading Researcher

Financial Analyst

Financial Consultant

Financial Manager

Financial Planner

Fund Accounting Manager

Institutional Equity Sales

Insurance Underwriter

Investment Broker

Junior Accountant

Legal Collector

Loan Administrator

Loan Executive

Loan Processor

Loan Servicer

Management Accountant

Marketing Representative

Mortgage Underwriter

Payroll Manager

Performance Measurement
Counsel

Project Manager

Quantitative Analyst

Quantitative International Equity
Trader

Report Developer

Securities Lending Trader

Senior Business Marketing
Analyst

Senior Business Planning and
Reporting Analyst

Senior Financial Services
Associate

Senior Organizational
Development Specialist

Senior Risk Analyst

Senior Systems Developer

Senior Systems Engineer

Staff Auditor

Stock Broker

Systems Developer

Tax Accountant

Tax Inspector

Team Leader

Team Manager

Vice President of Administration
and Finance

Vice President of Finance

RESUME BUZZ WORDS:

1099 Tax Information

A/P

A/R

Absorbing Cost

Abusive Tax Shelter

Accommodative Monetary Policy

Account Aggregation

Accounting

Accounting Software

Accounting Systems

Accounts

Accounts Payable

Accounts Receivable

Accredited Investor

Acid Test

Acquisitions

Actual Reports

Actuarial Department

Actuarial Valuation Report

Adjusted Gross Income

Administrative Leadership

ADP System

Advances

Affiliate

Affinity Investment Scheme

Allotment Needs

Alternative Investment Market

Analysis of Financial Data

Analytical Services

Annual Budget Process

Annual Budgets

Annual Capital Budgets

Annual Operations

Annuity

Appropriation of Money

Asset Management

Asset Reconciliation

Asset Responsibility

Assets

Audit Papers

Audit Requests

Audit Schedules

Auditing

Auditors

Audits

Automated Transmission Process

Balance of Trade

Balance Sheets

Bank Balances

Bank Reconciliations

Bank Training Program

Bar Charts

Bear Market

Bellwether Stock

Benefits Reports

Bids

Big Five

Big Three

Bill Payment

Billing Errors

Billing Systems

Black-Scholes Model

Blue Chip Stock

Board of Directors

Bond and Corporate Financial
    Services

Bond and Equity Transactions

Bond Market Association

Bonds

Bookkeeping

Boston Stock Exchange

Branch Office

Bridge Financing

Brokerage Firm

Brokerage License

Brokerage Services

Brokers

Budget

Budget Account

Budget and Investigated
    Variances

Budget Control

Budget Projections

Budgeting

Bull Market

Bureau of Economic Research
    (BEA)

Bureau of Labor Statistics (BLS)

Burn Basket Execution

Business Administration

Business Cycle

Business Development

Business Experience

Business Model

Business Plan

C.O.B.R.A.

Capital

Capital Budget

Capital Expenditure

Capital Gain

Capital Growth

Capital Surplus Statement

Cash

Cash Account

Cash Availability

Cash Disbursement

Cash Earnings

Cash Flow

Cash Management

CD's

Check Cashing Center

Check Disbursement

Check Verification

Checkbook Maintenance

Check-Cashing Center

Checks

Chicago Stock Exchange

Cincinnati Stock Exchange
(CIN)

Claim Liabilities

Claims Processing

Client Relations

Client's Asset Base

Close the Books

Closet Index

Coding of Receipts

Collections

Commerce Department

Commercial Credit Unions

Commercial Lending

Commercial Loan Operations

Commissions

Commodities

Commodity Futures

Commodity Options

Composite Index

Composite Table

Composite Yield

Compound Interest

Computer Models

Computer Systems

Consulting

Consumer Confidence Index
(CCI)

Consumer Credit

Contract Negotiation

Contract Proposals

Contractors

Contracts

Conversion Parity

Convertible Debt

Coordinated Payments

Corporate and Municipal
Securities

Corporate Banking Services

Corporate Clients

Corporate Finance

Corporate Financial Data

Corporate Financial Reporting

Corporate Lenders

Corporate Securities

Corporation Account

Cost Estimators

Cost of Living Adjustment
(COLA)

Credit Analysis

Credit Balance

Credit Bureau

Credit Reporting

Credit Terms

Currency

Custody Services

Customer Agreement

Customer Inquiries

Customer Relations

Customized Credit Solutions

Customized Investment Portfolios

Data Processing

Database Management

Day Trader

Debt

Debt Consolidation Services

Debt Underwriting

Decimal Pricing

Deferred Compensation Retirement Plan

Department of Commerce

Deposit Accounts

Derivatives

Derivatives and Asset Management

Devaluation

Development of a Mission

Direct Deposits

Director Labor and Standard Costs

Disbursement and Tracking of Loans

Disclosure Forms

Discount Brokerage

Discretionary Income

Discretionary Investment Management

Disposable Income

Divestiture

Dividend Credit

Dividend Receivables

Dividend Reinvestment Plan

Dividend/Interest Payments

Documentation

Dollar Bond

Donated Stock

Dow Jones Composite Average

Dow Theory

Due Diligence

Dynamic Pricing

Earned Surplus

Earnings Reports

Earnings Schedules

Earnings Season

Economic Indicators

Economics

EDP

Efficient Market Theory (EMT)

Emerging Markets

Employee Benefits Reports

Employer-Employee Relationships

Enforcement Policies

Equity

Equity Funds

Equity Ratio

E-Reporting

Escrow

Escrow Deposit

Estate Planning

Eurobonds

European Union (EU)

Exchange Rate

Excise Tax Laws and Regulations

Expenditures

Expense Recording

Expense Reports

Expenses

Federal/State/Unemployment
  Taxes

Filing Procedures

Finance

Financial Accounting

Financial Advisory Services

Financial Analysis

Financial Expertise

Financial Modeling

Financial Plan

Financial Reporting

Financial Statements

Financial Strategies

Financial Systems

Financial Trend Analysis

First and Junior Trust Deed
  Loans

Fixed Assets

Fixed Income Securities

Fixed-Income Sales and Trading

Fleet Financing

Flexible Funding Alternatives

Focus Sessions

Forecasts

Foreign Currency

Foreign Exchange

Foreign Markets

Fraud Account Functions

Fund Coding

Fund Custody Services

Fund Expenses

Fund/Sponsor Investments

Future Sales and Trading

GAAP and SSAP formats

GCAS Productivity

General Ledger

Global Fund Services

Global Macroeconomics

Global Markets

Global Trade Services

Government Entities

HMO Rates

Home Loans

Homeowners

Illustrative Cost Calculations

Income Statements

Income-Related Statements

Inequities

Information Systems

Institutional Equities

Insurance and Financial Services

Insurance Products

Integrated Financial Solutions

Internal Control Procedures

Internal/External Reporting

International Banking Services
International Bond Funds
International Economics
International Index Assets
Investment Banking
Investor Relations
Investor Services
Investors
Invoices
IRA
IRS Filing
IRS Service Policies
ISA/ABS Systems
Issuance of Policies
Journal Entries
Journal Transactions
Key Ratios
Leasing Companies
Legal and Credit Files
Lending
Liabilities
License Agreements
Lien Mortgage Loans
Line Management
Listed Companies
Loan Documents
Loan Payments
Lotus
Management Information
   Systems
Management Services

Managerial Accounting
Manual Worksheet System
Manually Issued Policies
Market Averages
Market Awareness
Market Indicators
Market Invoices
Marketing
Markets
Merchant Investment Banking
Mergers and Acquisitions
Middle- and Upper-Income
   Markets
Money Management
Money Market Account
Money Market Instruments
Month-End Journal
Monthly Closing
Monthly Financial Statements
Monthly Forecasts
Monthly Manufacturing
   Accounting Report
Mortgage Loans
Mortgages
Municipal Securities
Mutual Funds
NASD Regulations
NASDAQ
National/International Markets
New Benefits
New York Stock Exchange

Online Investments
Operating Budget
Operational Support
Options
Originating (Brokering and Funding)
Outstanding Payable Balance
Outstanding Tax Obligations
Overdrafts
Overdue Accounts
Partnerships
Past Due Interest
Payable Vouchers
Payroll
Payroll Coverage
Payroll Functions
Payroll Records
Personnel
Petty Cash
Planning Refinement
Portfolios
Premium-Based Worker's Compensation
Pricing Policies
Primary and Secondary Public Stock Offerings
Principal Auditor
Private Client Services
Private Companies
Probabilities
Problem Resolutions Skills

Production Costing
Profit Plans
Profit Sharing
Profitability
Pro-Forma Statements
Property and Casualty Carrier
Public Companies
Public Finance
Public Relations
Purchase Orders
Purchasing
Quantitative Analysis
Quarterly/Monthly Reports
Real Estate and Mortgage Loans
Real Estate Transactions
Receipts
Record Transactions
Recordkeeping Services
Regulators
Regulatory Bodies
Remit Payments
Reports
Repurchase Agreements
Residential Loan Applications
Retail Banking
Retirement Accounts
Retirement Management
Retirement Programs
Retirement Services
Retrospective Refund Liabilities

Revenue Collection

Royalties Computation

Sales

Schedules

SEC Reporting

Secured Business Lending

Secured Loan Programs

Securities

Securities Lending Services

Securities Services

Securities Trading

Security Discrepancies

Self-Insurance Program

Selling

Shareholder Account Activities

Shareholder Inquiries

Shares

Single Country Funds

Single-Family Residences

Spending Behavior

Spreadsheets

State Insurance Regulations and
  Legislation

Statistics

Stock Brokerage Licensure

Stock Market Investments

Stock Research

Stocks

Strategic Decisions

Strategic Plans

Tax and Insurance Escrow

Tax and Regulatory
  Requirements

Tax Filings

Tax Forms

Tax Liabilities

Tax Returns

Tax Shelters

Taxable Fixed Income

Tax-Deferred Investments

Tax-Exempt Assets

Telephone Collections

"Tiered" Interview Techniques

Trade Capture Settlement

Trade Management Development

Trade Settlements

Transaction Management

Transfers

Travel and Entertainment
  Reconciliations

Travelers Checks

Treasury

Treasury Bills

Trend Reports

Trial Balance

Trust and Banking Markets

Trust Departments

Unbillable/Uncollectible Business

Underwriting

Underwriting Philosophy

Underwriting Results

Valuation

Variable Annuity Products
Vendor Identification Files
Vendor Payments

Weekly Cash Requirements
Wire Transfers
Worker's Compensation

COMMONLY USED ACTION VERBS:

Acted	Created	Performed
Actuated	Determined	Planned
Adjusted	Developed	Posted
Administered	Entered	Prepared
Allocated	Established	Programmed
Analyzed	Estimated	Projected
Anticipated	Expanded	Provided
Appraised	Filed	Qualified
Assessed	Forecasted	Reconciled
Audited	Generated	Recorded
Balanced	Implemented	Reduced
Budgeted	Improved	Researched
Calculated	Maintained	Resolved
Compiled	Managed	Retrieved
Completed	Marketed	Reviewed
Composed	Measured	Settled
Computed	Monitored	Supported
Conserved	Netted	Utilized
Controlled	Oversaw	Worked
Corrected	Passed	

ACTION VERBS AND BUZZ WORDS USED IN CONTEXT:

• *Managed* all aspects of *finance, accounting, foreign exchange* dealings, *marketing*, and *data processing* of company and its overseas offices.

- *Reviewed* finances and securities pertaining to advances and shipping for client of about 200.

- *Audited* private companies; listed companies, partnerships, and individual business.

- *Prepared* financial statements and schedules.

- *Settled* bond and equity transactions in the United States markets.

- *Generated* income statements, balance sheets, general ledger, checks, and reports.

- *Entered* payable vouchers.

- *Performed* all accounting functions to include journal entries, accounts payable and receivable, petty cash, deposits, bank reconciliations, and trial balance.

- *Controlled* budget, cash flow, and capital expenditures.

- *Developed* corporate and project-oriented financial strategies.

CHAPTER TWO

ADMINISTRATIVE

THESE BUZZ WORDS ARE FOR applicants looking for general management and office positions. They reflect an involvement and familiarity with general office management as well as oversight of facilities and systems associated with the day-to-day organizational activities. Important skills include administrative, project management, customer service, and light labor.

COMMON POSITIONS INCLUDE:

Administrative Assistant	Order Entry Clerk
Administrative Director	Receptionist
Bank Teller	Secretary
Data Entry	Shipping/Receiving Expediter
Dispatcher	Staff Assistant
Executive Assistant	Stenographer
Executive Secretary	Telephone Operator
File Clerk	Ticket Agent
General Office Clerk	Typist
Inventory Control Analyst	Vice President of
Mail Room Supervisor	Administration
Office Manager	

Calculators

Certified Mail

Clerical Functions

Clerical Skills

...lacement

Client Files

Adding Machines

Client Relations

Administrative Policies and

Client/Customer Correspondence

    Procedures

Coding

Administrative Support Services

Commercial Loan Files

Advertising

Company Literature

Agendas

Computer and Software

Analysis

      Applications

Appraisal Files

Computer Operation

Archives

Computer Skills

Articulate/Expressive Speaker

Conferences

Associates Degree

Confidential Records

Association Membership

Contract Bids

Bank Services

Consultant

Banking Processes

Correspondence

Billing

Courier Services

Billing Systems

Credit Checks

Bills of Lading

Customer Inquiries

Bookkeeping

Customer Relations

Branch Audits

Customer Service

Budget Requirements

Daily Activities

Business Administration

Daily Deadlines

Business Forms

Daily Deliveries

Business Letters

Daily Fund Deposits

Busy Phone Work

Daily Office Functions

Daily Reporting

Data Entry

Data Gathering

Data Processing

Database Management

Departmental and Divisional
    Reports

Design Composition

Detail Oriented

Dictaphone

Direct Mail

Dispatch

Documentation

Donor Relations

Editing

E-mail

Employee Appraisals

Equipment Maintenance

Event Planning

Expense Accounts

Expense Reports

Express Mail

Facilities Management

Fax Messages

Federal Express

File Coding

File Maintenance

Filing Systems

Financial Management

Financial Statements

Forms

General Accounting Procedures

Human Resources

Inbound and Outbound Mail

Incoming Calls

Incoming Mail

Information Trafficking

Inquiry Resolution

Insurance Claims and Payments

Inter-Building Correspondence

Interviews

Inventory

Inventory Analysis

Inventory Control

Inventory Discrepancies

Inventory Systems

Invoicing

Logistics

Mail Processing

Marketing Forecast Reports

Mass Mailings

Material Coordination

Meeting Minutes

Meeting Planning

Meetings

Member Appointments

Membership

Merchandising

Monthly Charges

Monthly Payroll

Monthly Reports

Multiline Phones

Multiple Projects
Newsletter
Office Equipment
Office Management and
    Operations
Office Procedures
Office Reports
Online Database
Organization Policies and
    Procedures
Packing Slips
Payable Invoices
Periodical Production
Personnel Functions
Personnel Management
Personnel Records
Petty Cash
Phone Requests
Photo-Typesetting
Physical Inventory
Plan Meetings
Positive Attitude
Presentations
Press Releases
Problem Identification and
    Resolution
Problem Solving
Procedural Enhancement
Procedure Manual
Procedures
Processing

Product Displays
Production Schedules
Promotions/Contests
Proofreading
Public Inquiries
Public Relations
Purchase Orders
Questions and Complaints
Reconciliation
Record Keeping
Reference Library
Registered Mail
Relocation Policy
Report Generation
Report Writing
Reports
Research
Rules/Regulations
Sales Reports
Sales Support
Schedule Hours
Schedule Management
Secretarial Staff
Seminars
Shipping/Receiving
Shorthand
Site Visits
Special Events
Special Projects
Speed Writing
Spreadsheets

Staff Meetings
Staffing Needs
Statement Transcription
Statistical Typing
Statistics
Stenography
Strict Deadlines
Supervisory Skills
Survey Data
Switchboard
Systems Enhancement
Tax Returns
Telephone Inquiries
Telex
Time Records
Time Sheets

Trade Shows
Training Skills
Transcription
Travel Arrangements
Travel Calendar
Travel Vouchers
Troubleshooting
Typing
UPS
Vendor Relations
Word Processing
Words Per Minute (WPM)
Work Flow
Workers' Compensation
Writing Skills

COMMONLY USED ACTION VERBS:

Arranged
Assisted
Budgeted
Collected
Conducted
Coordinated
Created
Designed
Developed
Distributed
Edited
Executed
Facilitated

Filed
Handled
Implemented
Improved
Managed
Monitored
Organized
Performed
Planned
Prepared
Prioritized
Produced
Provided

Recorded
Resolved
Scheduled
Secured
Served
Serviced
Solicited
Sorted
Supervised
Tested
Translated
Utilized

Z WORDS USED IN CONTEXT:

into numerical code for *data entry*.

rchive.

hysical inventory procedures.

• *Served* as principal *consultant* on *plant inventory systems*.

• *Developed* nationwide *relocation policy* and *procedures* for new employees.

• *Provided* word processing, customer relations, and some *accounts payable processing*.

🖊 *Handled incoming calls*; *scheduled* appointments.

• *Supervised* employees to ensure observation of *rules/regulations*.

• *Provided customer service*; *resolved* complaints.

• *Coordinated* catering for *special events*.

• *Budgeted* and *facilitated* four-day professional *seminar*.

• *Secured* new business utilizing *customer inquiries* and *mass mailing* responses.

• *Scheduled site visits* and installations.

• *Collected*, *sorted*, and *distributed incoming mail*.

• *Created* effective *product displays*.

• *Monitored* equipment and supply *inventories*.

🖊 *Performed analysis* of *client files*.

CHAPTER THREE

AEROSPACE

POSITIONS IN THIS FIELD MIGHT

be in manufacturing, commercial or military aviation, or research. Aerospace industry buzz words display experience with manufacturing, engineering, and maintenance of commercial, military, and business aircraft; helicopters; aircraft engines; missiles; spacecrafts; and materials, related components, and equipment. This includes scientific research; hands-on work repairing and constructing aircraft equipment and parts; guaranteeing customer safety through quality assurance testing; and producing reliable, high-quality products.

COMMON POSITIONS INCLUDE:

Account Executive

Business Development
Manager

Cabin Crew Member

Contracts Manager

Database Analyst

Engineer

Engineered Product Support
Specialist

Enterprise Data Architect

Flight Deck Crew Member

Lead Stress Engineer

Managing Software Engineer

Manufacturing Planner

Material Handler
Materials and Process Engineer
Mechanical Engineer
Project Engineer
Risk Engineering Consultant
Sales Engineer
Scientist
Senior Aerodynamics Engineer
Senior Design Checker

Senior Quality Engineer
Senior Subcontracts
   Administrator
Systems Analyst
Technical Sales Leader
Test Engineer
Tool Facilities Operator
Vehicle Inspector

RESUME BUZZ WORDS:

ABS Resins
Acquisition Management
Activity Reports
Actuators
Adapter Cards
Advanced Combat Systems
Advanced Fighter Aircraft
Advanced Technology Products
Aerospace Defense Products
Aerospace Ordnance Devices
Aerospace Systems
Aerospace Telemetry
Air Defense Technologies
Air Force Material Command
Air Traffic Control
Air/Coastal Defense Radar
   Systems
Aircraft
Aircraft Avionics
Aircraft Components

Aircraft Engines
Aircraft Fuel Systems
Aircraft Fuselages
Aircraft Maintenance
Aircraft Modification
Aircraft Refueling
Altitude
Analysis Reports
Appliances
Audio Accessories
Automation
Aviation Communications
   Products
Avionic Display Systems
Avionic Mechanisms
B-2 Spirit Stealth Bomber
Boeing 747
Braking Control Systems
Broadcasting
Cabin Interior Products

Cabin Video Systems

Capital Services

Casting Foundry

Circuit Breakers

Circuits

Combat Systems

Command/Control Systems

Commercial Aircraft

Commercial Aircraft Parts

Commercial Jet Transports

Commercial Pumping Systems

Computer Bus Structures

Computer Peripheral

Computer Systems
   Development

Computer-Based Information

Control Equipment

Control Systems

Control Valves

Controls

Corporate Aircraft

Coupling Equipment

Data Communications Hardware
   Products

Data Interchange Services

Database Systems Support

Defense Industry

Defense Systems

Design Activities

Displacement and Pressure
   Transducers

Distribution of Electricity

Ducting Systems

Dynamic Hydraulic and
   Mechanical Testing

Dynamic Testing

Edge-Lighted Plastic Panels

Electric Motors

Electrical Components

Electrical Distribution

Electrical Modules

Electrical Supply Houses

Electromagnetic Parts

Electromechanical Locks

Electronic Components

Electronic Firing Systems

Electronic Industrial Automation
   Products

Electronic Systems

Electronics

Electro-Optics

Emergency Rescue Equipment

Energy Extraction Applications

Engine Components

Engine Instrumentation

Engine Parameters

Engines

Environmental Testing

Ethernet

Evaluation Reports

Executive Aircraft

Explosive Devices

External Commercial and
  Industrial Customers
F/A-18
Filters
Filtration Equipment
Fire Detection/Protection
  Systems
Flight Controls
Flight Simulators
Flight Test Data
Fluid Power Systems
Freight Air Carriers
Fuel
Fuel Pumps
Fusing Devices
General Aviation Aircraft
Global Support
Ground Support Services
Heavy Equipment
Helicopters
High-Security
High-Technology Ferrous
Hydraulic
Igniter Assemblies
Industrial Applications
Industrial Automation and
  Control
Industrial Gas Turbine Engines
Industrial Lighting Products
Industrial Machinery
Industrial Use

Inertial Navigation and Guidance
Information Systems
  Management
Inter-Computer Network
  Communications
Interior Aircraft Equipment
Jet Aircraft Engine Parts
Jet Engines
Laminates
Large Commercial Aircraft
Laser Firing Systems
Latching Devices
Light Machining
Liquid Propellant
Local Area Network
Logistics
Logistic Support Analyses
Major Aircraft Manufacturers
Manufacturing Methods
Manufacturing Support Services
Marine Systems
Measuring Methods
Mechanical Separation Devices
Medical Supplies
Medical Systems and Equipment
Microcircuits
Microelectronics
Microprocessor-Based Electronic
  Sequencers
Military Aircraft
Military Missiles

Military Planes
Missile Systems
Missiles
Molecular Biology Research Items
Nacelle Systems and Components
Navigation Control Systems
Navigational Instruments
Network Topologies
Networking Products
Nonferrous Castings
Operations Research
Optical Equipment
Optical Pick-Offs
Orbiting Satellites
Ordnance-Related Products
Panel Meters
Passenger Air Carriers
Passenger Control Units
Passenger Video Entertainment
    Systems
Performance Polymers
Plastics
Pneumatic Component Parts
Policies
Positioning Instruments
Power Cartridges
Power Systems
Precision Fastening Systems
Precision Measuring Scales
Precision Patterned Glass and
    Metal Products

Pressure Regulators
Pressure Transducers
Procedures
Processes
Product Development
Programming Experience
Pumps
Quality Assurance
Quality Control
Radar Equipment
Radio and Television
    Transmitters for Aircraft
Remote Network Access
    Communications
Repair Services
Replacement Parts
Resistors
Rocket Engines
Rotary and Linear Optical
    Incremental Encoders
Satellite Guidance Systems
Satellite-Based Communications
    Systems
Scientific Applications
Sensors
Service Accessories
Servovalves
Shared Services
Sheetmetal
Silicones
Simulation-Based Devices

Simulator-Related Training
Services
Small-Launch Vehicles
Software Systems
Solid Rocket Motors
Sophisticated Aerospace
Equipment
Sounding Rockets
Space
Space and Communications
Space and Aviation Systems
Space and Missile Systems Center
(SMC)
Space Applications
Space Systems Architecture
Space Vehicles
Specialty Insurance
Speed
Strategic Missile Systems
Strategic Weapon Systems
Superabrasives

Systems Analysis
Systems Engineering
Systems Management
Tactical Air Defense Systems
Tactical Missile Systems
Tactical Weapon Systems
Technical Guidance
Technical Products
Testing
Token Ring
Training Devices
Training Services
Transmission
Transportation Systems Products
Troubleshooting
Turbine Engines
Valves
Vibration (Random/Sine) Testing
Waterjet Propulsion Systems
Weapon Systems
Wiring Systems

COMMONLY USED ACTION VERBS:

Analyzed	Evaluated	Production
Assisted	Generated	Provided
Designed	Led	Recommended
Developed	Manufactured	Researched
Engaged	Performed	Supplied
Engineered	Planned	Tracked
Established	Prepared	Wrote

ACTION VERBS AND BUZZ WORDS USED IN CONTEXT:

- *Evaluated* quality-control *processes*, *policies*, and *procedures*.

- *Recommended* revisions of *weapons systems*.

- *Provided* technical guidance to staff of twenty; *tracked* progress of *product development*.

- *Wrote* analysis reports for the development of advanced *combat systems*.

- *Researched* and *generated* flight test data for company handbook focusing on *military planes* and *missile systems*.

- *Assisted* in the design of new and current *wiring systems*, *adapter cards*, and *positioning instruments*.

- *Designed* and *developed* manufacturing methods for *major aircraft manufacturers*.

- *Established* new operating *procedures* for the improvement of *industrial-use turbine engines*.

- *Prepared* evaluation reports, *performed* routine *quality-assurance* tests, and was involved in *troubleshooting network* failures.

- *Led* initial *design activities* and *assisted* in ground *product development* on a number of projects.

CHAPTER FOUR

APPAREL, FASHION, AND TEXTILES

BUZZ WORDS IN THIS INDUSTRY highlight experience with clothing design, export, and sales; knowledge of current style or style characteristics; or the manufacturing, weaving, and knitting of fabric, yarn, or cloth. This includes work with curtains, drapery, shoes, and sportswear; skill with nonwoven fabrics, textile goods and finishing, and yarn and thread mills; or the buying, handling, shipping, receiving, and selling of such goods.

COMMON POSITIONS INCLUDE:

Buyer	Outside Sales Representative
Converter	Patternmaker
Customer Sales Representative	Planner
Designer	Printer
Domestic Product Manager	Production Manager
Fashion Sales Representative	Quality Controller
Independent Sales Executive	Retail Store Manager
Merchandiser	Sampling Coordinator
Merchandising Manager	Senior Designer

Sewer Stitcher

Stylist

Technical Designer

Textile Tester

RESUME BUZZ WORDS:

Absorbency

Accent

Accessories

Acetate

Apparel

Apparel Design Arena

Apparel-Manufacturing
    Company

Apprenticeship

Artwork

Assortment

Automotive Distribution

Bandages

Baseball Caps

Bedroom Ensembles

Belts

Block and Slopers Development

Blouses

Brand Names

Brands

Bridal Gowns

Care Labels

Carpet

Casual Wear

Catalog Sales

Chain Stores

Chamois Flannel

Children's Sleepwear

Cloth Labels

Clothes

Clothing Manufacturers

Coats

Color

Comforters

Commission

Complete Line

Consumer Markets

Convert Fabric

Core Products

Cotton

Cotton-Blend Fibers

Curtains

Daywear

Denim

Department Store Merchandise

Design Concepts

Designer Jeans

Designer Lines

Designs

Detail

Die-Casting

Direct Marketing

Distribution Centers

Diversified Line

Divisions

Draperies

Dress Shirts

Dresses

Dye-Printing Process

Dyeing

Elastic Knitting

Export

Extensive Range

Eye Glasses

Fabrics

Fashion Apparel Products

Fibers

Filament

Finished Home Products

Footwear

Formal Wear

Furnishings

General Merchandise Stores

Global Retailer

Goods

Grade Rules

Half Sizes

Hand-Knitting Yarn

High-Quality Fabric

High-End Velvet

High-Spec Industrial
    Applications

Home Fashion Products

Home Furnishings

Import

Independent Textile Converter

Industrial Distribution

Industrial Hosiery

Industrial Markets

Industrial Processes

Industrial Uniforms

Interior Furnishings

Intimate Apparel

Inventory

Jackets

Jeans

Jersey Fabrics

Junior Sizes

Knit

Knit Health Care Products

Knitted Fabrics

Knitted Fleece

Knitted Textile Fabrics

Labels

Laces

Leather Apparel

Leisure Shirts

Leisurewear

Licensed Labels

Licenses

Licensing

Loungewear

Luggage

Lycra and Rubber Products

Mail Order Catalogs

Major Discounters

Man-Made Fibers

Manufacturers

Manufacturing Plants

Marketing

Markets

Mass Merchants

Mass Volume Retailers

Material

Measurement Charts

Medical Products

Men's Apparel

Merchandise

Metal and Coil Slide Fasteners

Micro Safe Fiber

Miss Sizes

Narrow Elastic Fibers

National and Regional Chains

Nationally Distributed

Natural and Synthetic Fibers

Neckwear

Nonwovens

Novelties

Nylon Fibers

Nylon Travelers

Outerwear Line

Packaging Products

Pants

Paper Making Machines

Patternmaking

Patterns

Petite

Petite Dresses

Pillows

Plaids

Plastic Injection Moldings

Polyurethane Coated Fabrics

Principal Buyers

Printed Fabrics

Printed Items

Private Label Sleepwear

Private Labels

Private Retail

Private-Label Designer

Processes Wool

Processing

Producing Pattern

Product Development

Production

Products

Purses

Quality Control

Retail Outlets

Retail Sales Prices

Retail Units

Retailers

Robes

Rug Kits

Sale

Sales Category

Samples

Scarves

Sewing Thread

Sheets

Shirts

Shoes

Skirts

Slacks

Special Machinery Spools

Special Occasion Dresses

Specialty Fabrics

Specialty Markets

Specialty Stores

Specialty Weaves

Spinning Cotton

Sportswear

Sportswear Items

Spun Yarns

Stores

Stretch Panties

Styles

Suits

Support Facilities

Synthetic

Synthetic Filament Polyester

Synthetic Thread

Tailored Men's Clothing

Tapes

Textile Outerwear

Textile Products

Textile Products Manufacturing

Textile Wholesaler

Textile Yarns

Textiles

Textured Nylon

Texturing

Towels

Trading

Trimmings

T-Shirts

Twisting

Undergarments

Uniform Shirts

Uniforms

Upholstery

Value-Priced Apparel

Variety

Warp Knit Fabrics

Washable Service Apparel

Watches

Wear

Weaving

Weekend Casual Sportswear

Wide-Warp Knit

Winding

Window Treatments

Women's Apparel

Women's Sheer Hosiery

Woodturnings

Woolen Coats

Worldwide

Woven

Woven Finished Fabrics

Woven Greige Fabrics

Woven Synthetics

Woven Velvets	Young Ladies'
Wrinkle-Free Cotton Fabrics	Young Men's Apparel
Yarns	Youth Market

COMMONLY USED ACTION VERBS:

Checked	Handled	Purchased
Created	Licensed	Received
Designed	Managed	Sold
Developed	Manufactured	Supervised
Established	Oversaw	Tailored
Featured	Printed	Wove
Finished	Processed	
Generated	Produced	

ACTION VERBS AND BUZZ WORDS USED IN CONTEXT:

• *Generated* high-quality *apparel* for major *brand name labels*. Responsibilities included keeping *inventory* of *specialty fabrics*, *sewing thread*, and *scarves*; contacting *retailers*; and updating *marketing* charts.

• *Supervised* workers in *apparel-manufacturing company*, specifically dealing with *product development* and *quality control*.

• Responsible for *handling* mail orders from *mass merchants* for *women's apparel*.

• *Developed* a *line* of *wrinkle-free cotton fabrics* with team of *textile* engineers while working in an experimental-based *apparel design arena*.

• *Oversaw patternmaking* process, from initial *design concept* through *woven finished fabrics*.

- *Checked* samples for *texturing* and *fiber* consistency.

- *Designed* metal and coil slide fasteners for *woolen coats.*

- *Produced* textile yarns, textured nylon, spun yarns, and knitted *textile fabrics* for company focused on *specialty weaves.*

- Responsible for the *purchasing* and *receiving* of *young ladies'* and *young men's clothing* at a *youth market retailer.*

- *Managed* specialty store that featured *intimate apparel, private label sleepwear,* and *high-end velvet accent furnishings. Featured* an assortment of *brand names; established* strong professional relationship with several major *retailers.*

- *Wove* textile yarns using *special machinery spools* for *private label designer.*

- *Tailored* men's dress slacks, shirts, jackets, and *formal wear* under *apprenticeship.*

- *Established* dye-printing process for *generating* plaid patterns on *high-quality fabrics.*

- *Created* designer line of *women's purses, shoes,* and *accessories.*

- *Sold* lycra and rubber products to major *sportswear* producers worldwide.

CHAPTER FIVE

ARCHITECTURE, CONSTRUCTION, AND ENGINEERING

IN THESE FIELDS, EFFECTIVE buzz words highlight one's experience with applying scientific and mathematical principles to the design, layout, and construction of machines, structures, buildings, and systems. This includes planning the physical composure of a bridge, house, or monument; graphically conceptualizing the mathematical dynamics of huge land structures; and physically preparing, assembling, or renovating pre-existing architecture.

COMMON POSITIONS INCLUDE:

Architect	Estimator
Bridge Department Manager	Foreman
Campus Planning Leader	Graphics Support Specialist
Chief Transportation Planner	Highway Design Engineer
Civil Designer	Landscape Architect
Civil Engineer	Lead Mechanical Estimator
Electrical Engineer	Project Architect
Engineer	Project Designer

Railway Signal Design Engineer

Senior Interior Designer

Senior Project Designer

Steward

Surveyor

Team Leader

Transportation Planning
 Engineer

Urban Design Principal

RESUME BUZZ WORDS:

Accident Reconstruction

Accident Statistical Data Analysis

Aggregates

Air Conditioning Systems

Airfield Lighting Power
 Distribution

Airfields

Airports

Architectural Planning

Architectural/Engineering
 Services

Asphalt Felt-Based Linoleum

Asphalt Paving

Aviation

Banks

Biomechanics

Brick Masonry

Bridge Inspection

Bridges

Budget Development

Builders

Building Entrances

Building Materials

Building Plans

Building Products

Building Restoration

Buildings

Business Support Services

Cabinets

Carpet Base

Chemicals

Civic Centers

Civil Disciplines

Civil Engineering

Coal

Coal Production

Code Compliance

Commercial Architecture

Commercial Construction

Commercial Industries

Commercial Services

Compressor/Vacuum Pump
 Products

Computer Aided Design (CAD)

Conceptual Design

Concrete Repair

Condominiums

Construction

Facilities and Transportation

Facings

Feasibility Studies

Federal Programs

Field Crews

Field Engineering and Inspection

Field Experience

Field Reports

Field Responsibilities

Financing Operations

Fire/Life Safety Design

Fittings

Floor Adhesives

Flooring

Flooring Products

Frame Parts

General Contracting Firm

General Contractor

Geotechnical Investigation

Geotechnical Services

Global Services

Government Bases

Graphics

Hard Floor Coverings

Hazardous Waste Assessment and
    Remediation

Heating and Air-Conditioning
    Equipment

Heating Systems

Heavy Construction

Heavy Industrial Construction

Heavy Rail

Heavy-Civil Contractor

Highway Capacity

Highway Contractor

Highways

Homebuilders

Hospitality Projects

Hotels

Industrial Complexes

Industrial Facilities

Infrastructure Systems

Interior Design Services

Job Site Management Team

Labor Units

Laboratories

Land Planning

Lateral and Axial Pile Analyses
    Programs

Lav-Tops

Layout

Leading Mortgage Finance
    Company

Lighting Control and Monitoring
    System

Lighting Products

Loss-Control Services

Maintenance Services

Major Bridges

Major Cargo Airports

Management Consulting

Manufacturing Industry

Marine Facilities
Marine Investigations
Material Take-Off
Materials and Product Testing
Mechanical Contracting
Mechanical Design Drawings
Mechanical Estimates
Mechanical Subcontracting
Metal Fabrication Services
Metal Siding
Metals
Minerals
Monitor Panels
Multidisciplinary Approach
Multifaceted Construction
    Firm
Multifamily Apartment
    Complexes
Nonresidential Architectural
    Building Products
Nuclear Fuel
Occupancies
Office Buildings
Operating Groups
Operation and Construction
    Management Services
Pavement
Petrochemical Industry
Petroleum Refining
Pharmaceuticals and
    Biotechnologies Industries

Piping Pricing
Piping Takeoffs
Planning
Plumbing
Plumbing Supplies
Policyholders
Pollution Control
Polymers
Power Distribution
Pre-cast Concrete
Prevention of Accidents and
    Failures
Private Sectors
Probable Risk Assessment
Procurement
Procurement Management
Professional Services
    Organization
Programming
Project Conception
Project Planning
Project Team
Properties
Protection of Traffic Plan
    Development
Public Facilities
Public Sectors
Public Works
Pulp
Quality Control
Quantity Estimates

Quantity Takeoff Calculations

Railroads

Railway Signal Engineering
    Designs

Range Hoods

Ready-Mixed Concrete

Real Estate Agencies

Refrigeration Contractor

Related Mobile Home
    Products

Relevant Codes

Remediation Services

Remote Site Camps

Renovation

Research Laboratories

Residential

Residential Building
    Maintenance Services

Restoration

Risk Prevention/Mitigation

Road/Highway

Roof Domes

Roof Vents

Roofing

Safeguard the Environment

Semiconductor

Sheet Metal Fabrication

Siding

Single-Family Homes

Slope Stability Modeling
    Programs

Solar Energy Components

Solid Waste

Spatial and Statistical Analysis

Specialists

Specialty Construction Services

Specialty Sheets of Foam

Specifications

Sports Facilities

Sprinkler and Irrigation
    Products

Steel Industry

Storefronts

Streets

Structural Concrete
    Construction

Structural Engineering

Structural Projects

Stucco

Subcontractors

Suppliers

Surety Claim Services

Surveying

System Safety and Reliability

Task Areas

Technical Consulting

Technical Presentations of
    Proposals

Tenant Improvements

Tile

Toplights

Total Engineering

Traffic

Traffic Signal Design and
   Maintenance

Training

Transition Strip Accessories

Transportation

Transportation Markets

Transportation Model Network
   Coding

Transportation Related

Tunnels

Value Management

Valves

Ventilation

Warning and Labeling Issues

Waste Management

Wastewater Collection

Wastewater Reuse

Wastewater Treatment

Water Management

Water Resources

Water Treatment and
   Distribution

Water/Wastewater Services

Waterfront Facility

Wide-Ranging Climates

Window Framing

COMMONLY USED ACTION VERBS:

Built	Drew	Proposed
Completed	Generated	Renovated
Conceptualized	Managed	Researched
Conducted	Outlined	Scheduled
Constructed	Oversaw	Served
Controlled	Planned	Supervised
Designed	Prepared	Surveyed
Drafted	Programmed	Transported

ACTION VERBS AND BUZZ WORDS USED IN CONTEXT:

• *Prepared* and *completed* residential building maintenance services.

• *Scheduled* and *supervised* work of *project team* members on *transportation model network coding*.

- *Oversaw* work delegated to *subcontractors* for *public sectors*.

- *Served* as an *engineer* on *railroad signal engineering designs*, *traffic signal designs*, and *wastewater treatment* teams.

- *Transported* supplies to *field crewmembers* from *construction base*.

- *Conducted* accident statistical data analysis for all *warning and labeling issues*.

- *Constructed* sports facilities, railroads, and bridges and worked on *building restorations* during more than twenty years of *construction* and *foreman* work.

- Skilled in *computer aided design (CAD)*, *layout*, and *programming* for intricate *building plans*.

- Experienced in *roofing, window framing, tiling, siding, flooring*, and *renovation*.

- *Managed* architectural projects from *conceptual design* to completion.

CHAPTER SIX

ARTS, ENTERTAINMENT, SPORTS, AND RECREATION

THESE BUZZ WORDS ARE JUST some of those from the often glamorous worlds of entertainment, sports, and arts; each individual field within these industries will have many more specific terms that might be used to demonstrate your knowledge and experience. Arts resume buzz words display experience with production or arrangement of sounds, colors, forms, movements, or other visual elements. (Chapter Thirty, focusing on working artists in the visual and performing arts, has more buzz words for these fields.) Entertainment industry buzz words exhibit experience producing performances or shows to amuse, please, or divert an audience's attention. Entertainment buzz words also display experience working for studios, networks, production companies, record companies, and radio stations. Sports and recreation buzz words highlight experience with both competitive and relaxing activities such as games and matches.

COMMON POSITIONS INCLUDE:

Account Executive
Administrative Assistant
Art Director
Athletics Director
Booking Specialist
Business Affairs Assistant
Contract Assistant
Designer
Desktop Publisher
Event Associate
Fashion Stylist
Feature Producer
Graphic Designer
Inventory Analyst
Licensed Cosmetologist
Makeup Artist
Marketing Specialist

Music and Development
    Assistant
Photographer
Producer
Product Development and
    Production Supervisor
Production Coordinator
Program Director
Promotions Assistant
Publicist
Publicity Coordinator
Research Analyst
Sales Manager
Tele-Sales Representative
Ticket Services Representative
Writer

RESUME BUZZ WORDS:

360-Degree Theater Systems
Action/Adventure Films
Actor Management
Amusement Park
Ancient Art
Animation
Arcade
Art Department
Art Media
Awards Shows

Background
Ballets
Banquet Facilities
Botanic Gardens
Broadcasting
Broadway Theaters
Cable Television
    Networks
Cardiovascular Equipment
Casinos

CD Manufacturing and Distribution Facility

CD-audio and CD-ROM Mastering and Replication

Children's Cartoons

Circus

Coaching Staff

Comedic Theater

Comedy Films

Concerts

Concession Facilities

Conservation and Curatorial Departments

Contracted Artists

Convention and Meeting Facility

Dance

Digital Effects

Digital Images

Director Management

Discovery Labs

Documentary

Editing, Design, Sound, and Related Services

Education Services

Educational and Research Programs

Entertainment

Entertainment Production Company

Event Television

Exercise Programs

Exhibition Halls

Family Audiences

Fashion

Feature-Length Motion Pictures

Fellowships

Film Development

Film Distribution Company

Film-to-Tape and Tape-to-Film Transfer

Finishing

First-Run Syndication

Fitness and Aerobic Classes

Fitness Center

Foreign Television Networks

Free Television

Fulfillment Services

Full-Service Health and Fitness Club

Giant Screen

Guest Hotel Facilities

Hair

Harness Racing Facility

Hiking Trails

Historic Artifacts

Historical Interpretation

History Museum

Home Video

Horseracing Tracks

Independent Multimedia Manufacturing

Integrated Merchandising

Intellectual Property Rights

Interactive Games

Interactive Media

Internships

Laser Disc Licensees and
    Distributors

Laser Video Disc Recording

Layout

Lectures

Leisure and Entertainment
    Company

Libraries

Licensing

Live Animals

Live Entertainment

Low-Budget Theatrical Motion
    Pictures

Made-for-TV Movies

Magazines

Makeup

Manuscripts

Media Company

Meets

Merchandising

Miniseries

Modern Art

Motion Picture Business

Motion Picture Film Processing

Motion Pictures

Museums

Music Production

National and International Tours

National Basketball Association
    (NBA)

National Football League (NFL)

National Hockey League (NHL)

Major League Baseball (MLB)

Nature Center

Newspapers

Nonprofit Art Gallery

Nonprofit Arts Showcase

Nonprofit Cultural Organization

Nonprofit Performing Arts
    Theater

Off-Broadway

Off-Line and Online Video
    Editing

On-Broadway

Online Services

Opera

Opera House

Orchestra

Outdoor Activity Programs

Packaging

Paddle Boats

Parks

Pay Television

Performing Arts Facility

Personal Training

Photo Finishing

Pipeline

Political Satire

Popular and Classical Records

Portable Simulator

Practice

Preservation of Buildings and
   Ships

Production Planning

Professional Hockey

Professional Resident Theater
   Company

Professional Sports Teams

Prospecting

Publications and Reproductions

Publishing

Puppetry

Recreation Program

Regional Cable Television Sports
   Networks

Research Library

Revisualization Sequences

Rights to Films

Roller Skating Rink

Satellite Transmission Uplinking
   Services

Schedules

Set Dressing

Shakespearean Productions

Sitcoms

Snack Bar

Special Effects

Special Interest Programming

Special Productions

Sports Highlights

Stakes Races

State-of-the-Art Theaters

Student Art Exhibitions

Studio Facilities and Technology

Syndicates

Talent and Literary Agency

Talk Shows

Tanning

Television Programs

Theatrical Exhibitions

Theatrical Performances

Toy Design

Type Design

Uniforms

Vaudeville

Venues

Video and Film Duplication

Video Post-Production Services

Video Theater

Videocassette and Audiocassette
   Duplication

Virtual Reality Theater Systems

Visual Arts Museum

Warehousing

Water Theme Park

Websites

Weights

Women's National Basketball
   Association (WNBA)

Women Viewers

COMMONLY USED ACTION VERBS:

Acted	Developed	Planned
Analyzed	Directed	Produced
Competed	Managed	Promoted
Conceptualized	Organized	Provided
Created	Oversaw	Supervised

ACTION VERBS AND BUZZ WORDS USED IN CONTEXT:

• *Managed* high-profile *art department*, which included a large staff, freelance *designers*, and outside vendors.

• *Catalogued* 250 *images* to silhouette, using soft-edge to masque and feather to clear the *background*.

• *Provided animation* to other departments (*set dressing*, *layout*, etc.) as needed during their phases of *production*.

• *Conceptualized*, *created*, and *analyzed digital media images*, *type design*, and *motion design* for DVD and *broadcast video*.

• *Planned* and *organized practices* and *meets*; taught swimming technique; kept *schedules*, equipment, and *uniforms* organized.

• *Planned*, *organized*, *directed*, and *promoted* a comprehensive *recreation program* for the town that included a six-week summer youth program.

• *Developed* and *managed* department budget; *supervised* administrative, *athletic training*, and *coaching* staffs; *oversaw* scheduling of *recreation* activities.

CHAPTER SEVEN

AUTOMOTIVE

BUZZ WORDS FOR THE AUTO-
motive industry highlight experience in repair
shops and with producing automotive equipment and
knowledge of auto sales and services.

COMMON POSITIONS INCLUDE:

Aftermarket General Agent	National Sales Trainer
Automotive Engineer	National Technical Service
Automotive Field	Center Leader
Representative	Parts and Accessories Sales
Automotive Tech Line	Leader
Specialist	Parts Counter Person
Body Shop Manager	Parts Manager
Car Salesperson	Service Advisor
Dealer Consultant	Service Director
General Manager	Service Manager
Instructional Designer	Used Car Manager
Marketing Representative	Warranty Administrator
Mechanic	

RESUME BUZZ WORDS:

Accessories

Air Conditioners

Air Filters

Air Injection

Airbag Electronics

Airbags

Alignment

Alloy Wheels

All-Wheel Drive

Aluminum Bodies

Antilock Braking Systems (ABS)

Antilock Brakes

Assemblies

Assembly Services

Auctions

Auto Body Parts

Auto Reconditioning

Automatic

Automobile Doorframes

Automobile Parts

Automotive

Automotive Aftermarket

Automotive Design

Automotive Electronic Controls

Automotive Electronics

Automotive Glass

Automotive Occupant Restraint
    Systems

Automotive Parts

Automotive Regulators

Automotive Roll Form Products

Automotive Seating Systems and
    Components

Automotive Service

Automotive Starting Systems

Automotive-Original Equipment

Axles

Ball Bearings

Bimodal Vehicles

Blow Moldings

Body Stampings

Book Value

Brake Linings

Brake Pads

Brakes

Brazed Assemblies

Bus Specialty

Bushings

Caliper

Camping Trailers

Car Stereos

Cars

Certified Automotive Parts
    Supplier

Chassis

Chemicals

Child and Infant Seats

Climate-Control Systems

Clutch

Clutch Plates

Coatings

Coils

Combined Markets

Combustion Chamber

Commercial Vehicles

Compressor

Connecting Rod

Continuous-Strand Fiberglass

Contract Manufacturing Services Solutions

Conversion Facility

Conversion Van

Convertible Systems

Coolant

Coolant Systems Pressure Gauges

Custom Vehicles

Custom-Designed

Customers

Customizes

Cylinder Head

Cylindrical

Dealers

Decorative Laminates

Delivery Vehicles

Design

Development

Diesel Engines

Differential

Displays

Distributor

Domestic

Door Systems

Driveshaft

Drivetrain Components and Systems

Dry Freight Vans

Electric Automotive Switches

Electric Motors

Electrical

Electrical Automotive Equipment

Electrical Power Distribution Equipment

Electronic Controls

Electroplating

Engine Components

Engine Mounts

Engine Parts

Engineering Services

Exhaust

Exhaust Systems

Exterior Automobile Mirrors

Exterior Enhancement Programs

Extruded Plastic Materials

Fabricated Glass

Factory Equipment

Fifth Wheels

Financing

Flat Glass Products

Flat Tire

Flatbed Trailers

Floor Consoles

Fluid Connectors

Fluid Power

Fluid Systems Components

Four Wheel Drive

Frames

Franchised Auto Dealerships

Franchised Automotive Service
Locations

Front Wheel Drive

Fuel Filters

Fuel Injection

Fuel Injectors

Fuel Pumps

Fuel Systems

Fuel-Carrying Systems

Fuel-Handling Products

Full-Line Vehicle Manufacturers

Full-Size Vans

Fully Loaded

Gaskets

Generating Systems

Halogen Headlamp

Headlights

Heaters

Heavy Truck Chassis

Heavy Trucks

Heavy Vehicle Systems

Heavy-Duty Trucks

Hoses

Hydraulic Power Units

Hydraulic Products

Hydraulic Pumps

Ignition Systems

Import

Independent Supplier

Independent Suspension

Industrial Products

Inflatable Restraints

Information Technology

Injection Moldings

Inspections

Instrument Clusters

Instrument Panel Components

Interior Automotive Products

Interior Trim

Iron Castings

Latch Assemblies

Light Truck Seating Systems and
Components

Light Trucks

Light Vehicle Aftermarket

Light Vehicle Systems

Lighting Products

Lighting Systems

Limited Slip Differential

Maintenance

Manual

Manufactured Goods

Mass Transit

Metal Automobile Components

Metal Stampings

Mid-Range Diesel Engines

Midsize/Luxury Car Group

Mini Motor Homes

Minivans

Miscellaneous Automobile Parts

Molded Materials

Molded Plastics

Motor Coaches

Motorhomes

Motors Insurance

Octane Reading

Off-Road Machinery

Oil Caps

Oil Changes

Oil Filters

Options

Original Equipment
    Manufacturers (OEM)

Overdrive

Overhead System Components

Oxygen Sensors

Park Models

Parts

Passenger Cars

Pickup Truck Bedliners

Pickup Trucks

Pinion Steering Gears

Pistons

Piston Rings

Plastic Fasteners and Clips

Plastic Injection Molding

Plastic Interior Items

Plastic Products

Plastics

Pneumatic Products

Ports

Power Rack

Power Units

Powertrain

Powertrain Components

Powertrain Systems

Precision Parts

Precision Stamping

Product Design

Production Facilities

Push Rod

Quarter Panel

Radiator Pumps

Radiator Valves

Radiators

Recreational Vehicle
    Manufacturers

Recreational Vehicles

Refined Motor Cars

Refrigerated Trailers

Related Components

Rental

Replacement Parts

Replacement Parts Distribution

Research and Development
    (R&D)

Residual

Resins

Resonator

Ride-Control Products

RV

Safety Restraint Products

Sale

Sales/Service Groups

Sales-Automotive Aftermarket

Sealing

Seals

Seat Belts

Seats

Sectors

Sedans

Sensors

Service Centers

Service Operations

Shims

Sleeve Bearings

Small Car Group

Specialized Applications

Specialized Fibers

Specialized Truck Bodies

Spoilers

Sport-Utility Vehicles (SUV)

Standard Transmission

Steering Linkage

Strut

Sun Visors

Sunroofs

Supplies

Suspension

Suspension Ball Joints

Suspension Parts

Suspension Systems

Tail Lamps

Tapered Roller Bearings

Test Drive

Testing

Thrust Washers

Tier One Supplier

Tier Two Supplier

Timing

Tinted Glass Products

Tires

Tool Building Services

Tooling Applications

Torque

Traction Control

Tractors

Trailer Hitches

Transmission Bands

Transmission Parts

Transportation Manufacturing
    Firm

Travel Trailers

Trimming

Truck Bodies

Truck Campers

Truck Doorframes

Truck Drivetrain Systems

Truck Group

Trucks	Vehicle Transport Services
Tune Up	Vehicular Lighting Products
Turbocharger	Vibration Control Parts and
Universal Joint	Systems
Upscale Model	Washers
Used Cars	Welded Assemblies
Valve Train	Wheel Base
Valves	Wheels
Van Bodies	Wholesale Distribution
Van Campers	Wholesale Value
Vehicle Development Groups	Windows
Vehicle Leasing	Worldwide Markets
Vehicle Parts	

COMMONLY USED ACTION VERBS:

Accessorized	Explained	Produced
Assessed	Formed	Repaired
Built	Improved	Replaced
Certified	Installed	Serviced
Customized	Managed	Showed
Diagnosed	Manufactured	Sold
Distributed	Ordered	
Drove	Performed	

ACTION VERBS AND BUZZ WORDS USED IN CONTEXT:

• *Customized* automobiles, **installed** *tinted glass products, sunroofs, spoilers, halogen headlamps*, and related products.

• *Showed* cars, trucks, and *sport-utility vehicles* to potential customers; went on *test drives*, **explained** features on all *vehicles*, from basic to *fully loaded* models.

- *Performed* *maintenance* on all types of *vehicles*, including changing *oil filters*, *ordering* and *replacing* miscellaneous *parts*, and *repairing suspension systems*.

- *Managed* *auto* *parts* store, *selling* all *automotive* products from *tires* to *radiator pumps*.

- *Diagnosed* problems with *automobiles* brought in, assessed cost and timeframe of repair.

- *Produced* top of the line safety devices, such as *antilock braking systems*, *seat belts*, and *airbags*.

- *Manufactured* automotive electronic controls and *electrical power distribution equipment*.

- *Formed* molded plastics and precision stamping equipment.

- *Serviced* dozens of cars daily, mainly *performed tune-ups*, *oil changes*, and *inspections*.

- *Distributed* custom-designed auto body parts to *service centers* and specialty stores.

CHAPTER EIGHT

BIOTECHNOLOGY AND PHARMACEUTICALS

THE BUZZ WORDS IN THESE industries are often highly technical, and they exhibit a science background with in-depth familiarity of biology and chemistry. Resumes may demonstrate experience with cell biology, vaccine research, prescription drugs, over-the-counter medicines, chemical compounds used in pharmaceuticals, and tools used to diagnose diseases. Relevant experience includes synthesizing new drugs, testing of drugs, determination of dosages and delivery forms (such as liquid or tablets), calculating cost-effectiveness of a proposed drug, and selling/marketing of pharmaceuticals.

COMMON POSITIONS INCLUDE:

Account Manager	Biochemist
Administrative Assistant	Chemistry Scientist
Analyst	Clinical Lab Scientist
Application Chemist	Clinical Research Manager
Auditor	Consultant
Billing Coordinator	Customer Service Assistant

Customer Service Supervisor

Customer Service Technician

Engineer

Health/Safety Manager

Marketing Director

Mechanical Maintenance
Specialist

Medical Director

Physicist

Program Manager

Quality Control Specialist

Reimbursement Manager

Research Technician

Route Service Representative

Sales Assistant

Sales Associate

Scientist

Shipping and Receiving Clerk

Technician

RESUME BUZZ WORDS:

Advanced Cellular and Molecular
Biology

Agricultural Biotechnology

Allergies

Analytical Tools

Anemia

Antibodies

Antiviral

Aqueous-Based Synthetic
Solutions

Aseptic Processing Design

Assay (ELISA) Test Kits

Autoimmune

Bioinformatics

Biomedical Research

Biopharmaceutical Development

Biopharmaceutical Fermentation

Biosciences

Biostatistics

Biotechnology

Blood Management Systems

Blood Tests

Bone Marrow Transplantation

Breakthrough Drug

Calibration Programs

Cancer Research

Cardiovascular Disease

Cell Biology

Cell Lines

Cell-Based Functional Secondary
and Tertiary Assays

Centrifuges

Chemical Manufacturing

Chemotherapeutic
Pharmaceuticals

Clean Room Certification

Clinical Laboratories

Clinical Laboratory Services

Clinical Trials

Clinics

Cohort Studies

Compliance

Compound Screening

Computer Validation

Computerized System Validation

Contract Research Organization (CRO)

Contract Sales Organization (CSO)

Critical Care Products

Cultured Primary Cells

Data Analysis

Data Processing Software

Data Sets

Dermatology

Detection and Measurement Equipment

Development and Consulting

Diabetes

Diagnostic Analysis

Diagnostic Imaging

Diagnostic Medical Devices

Diagnostic Tests

Dialysis Centers

Direct-to-Consumer (DTC) Marketing

DNA Synthesizers

Donor Center

Dosing

Double-Blind

Drug Delivery Systems and Technologies

Drug Discovery

Drug Optimization Programs

Drug Strategies

Education

Electrophoresis Systems

Engineering Sciences

Environmental Monitoring Programs

Environmental Testing

Enzymatically Dissolved Hair Samples

Enzyme-Linked Immunosorbent

Epidemiological Issues

Epidemiological Research

Epidural Anesthesia

Ethical Pharmaceuticals

FDA Approval

FDA Compliance Strategies

Formulary

Gas Chromatography/Mass Spectrometry

Gene Therapies

General Chemical Systems

Generic Drug

Genetics

Genomics

Gerontological Studies

GMP Audits

Good Manufacturing Practices (GMP)

Government and Private Industry Research

Grant Proposals

Growth Deficiency Treatment

Health and State Policy

Health Care Policy

Health Inequalities and Disparities

Health Insurance

Hematology

Hormones

Human Genetic Information

Human Therapeutics

Humanized and Human Monoclonal Antibodies

IC50/ED50 Values

Immunoassays

Immunodiagnostic Products

Immunological Reagents

Immunology

Impact Research Programs

In Vitro

In Vitro Pharmacology Assays

In Vivo

Industrial Microbiology

Infectious Diseases

Intravenous Systems and Solutions

Inventory Management

Investigational New Drug Application (IND)

IQ, OQ, and PQ Protocols

IV Accessories

Laboratories

Large-Scale Surveys

Life Science Systems

Life Sciences

Longitudinal Analysis

Manufacturing Regulations

Measurement and Analysis of Physiologic Data

Medical Affairs

Medical Conditions

Medical Immunodiagnostic Test Kits

Metabolic Diseases

Metabolism

Metabolites

Multidisciplinary Research

Natural Growth Conditions

New Drug Application (NDA)

Observational Studies

Ophthalmic Pharmaceuticals

Ophthalmology

Organ Preservation Solutions

Organ Transplantation

Outsourcing Services

Over-the-Counter Drug (OTC Drug)

Patented Drug

Patient Care

Patient-Specific Intravenous Drugs

Pharmaceutical Companies

Pharmaceutical Devices

Pharmaceutical Discovery

Pharmaceutical Products

Pharmaceuticals

Pharmacy Services

Phase I

Phase II

Phase III

Pipeline

Placebo-Controlled Protocol

Plasma Exchange

Plasma Expanders

Preclinical Stage Programs

Public Health Research

Quality Control/Quality Assurance (QC/QA)

Quantitative Analysis

Reagents

Recombinant DNA

Regulatory Affairs

Regulatory Issues

Reproductive Disorders

Research and Clinical Applications

Research Methodologies

Retrospective Studies

Robotic Workstations

Scientific Instruments

Side Effects

Social Determinants of Illness

Social Research

Specialty Chemical Systems

Sterilization Processes

Surveillance

Testing for Acute and Chronic Human Illnesses

Therapeutic Systems

Thyroid Disorders

Tissue and Organ Replacement

Treatment for Life-Threatening Diseases

U.S. Food and Drug Administration (FDA)

Urine Tests

Urology/Gynecology Studies

Vaccines

Validation

Veterinary Applications

COMMONLY USED ACTION VERBS:

Applied	Coordinated	Directed
Compared	Designed	Discovered
Contributed	Determined	Disseminated

Facilitated	Leveraged	Provided
Generated	Maintained	Received
Guided	Managed	Sampled
Identified	Performed	Tracked
Implemented	Planned	Trained
Labeled	Processed	Utilized

ACTION VERBS AND BUZZ WORDS USED IN CONTEXT:

• *Contributed* to the discovery and *preclinical* development of *antiviral compounds*.

• *Designed* and *implemented in vitro* and *in vivo drug metabolism* and *pharmacokinetic experiments* to *facilitate* the selection and optimization of drug candidates.

• *Identified* potential *metabolites* by using state-of-the-art technologies from *in vitro* and *in vivo studies*.

• *Performed* tasks that support *study conduct*, according to all applicable regulations and operations procedures.

• *Utilized* and *maintained* standard *Medical Affairs* tracking tools.

• *Performed* initial review of *regulatory* and required study documents.

• Responsible for *inventory management* of nonclinical supply materials.

• *Applied* knowledge of *therapeutic* area and drug development (investigational, observational, *surveillance*).

• *Trained* others on job-related functions.

Chapter Nine

Communications

INDUSTRY BUZZ WORDS IN the area of communications highlight writing, graphics, public relations, publicity, and promotions skills and experience. This includes activities associated with creating, distributing, and transmitting text and graphic information via varied print, video, audio, computer, and Web-based media. Some of the buzz words below concerning editing and writing would also be useful for those applying for positions in publishing (see Chapter Twenty-Two for more words from that field).

Common Positions Include:

Account Manager	Editorial Director
Assistant Editor	Events Planner
Associate Editor	Information Support Specialist
Author	Journalist
Broadcast Producer	Knowledge Base Editor
Columnist	Managing Editor
Copy Editor	Online Commerce Designer
Correspondent	Payroll Assistant
Editor	Producer

Production Editor

Production Manager

Project Leader

Proofreader

Public Relations Practitioner

Publicist

Radio Announcer

Radio Program Director

Reporter

Research Analyst

Staff Writer

Symposium Coordinator

Technical Producer

Television Director

Television Producer

Television Production Engineer

Translator

Typesetter

Writer

Resume Buzz Words:

Acquisition of Titles

Administrative Skills

Advertising

Annual Fact Book

Antenna Designs and
Measurements

Art and Production Elements

Arts and Entertainment

Articles

Assignments

Asynchronous Transfer Mode
(ATM)

Audio Production

Authors

Automatic Call Distributors

Automation Solutions

Backlist

Blemishes

Book Production

Booklets

Broadcasting Operations

Business Presentations

Cable Television

Call Center Management

Call Centers

Camera Operation

Campaign Letters

Casting Contracts

Catalogs

CDs

Cellular Phones

Circulation Records

Classified Advertisings

Collaboration

Columns

Commercials

Communications Intelligence
Collection

Communications Management

Communications Service
  Provider

Communications Systems

Computer-Telephony Integration
  Solutions

Consumer Markets

Content

Content Development

Contributing Writers

Copyedit

Corporate Imaging

Cover Story

Creative Writing

Darkroom Procedures

Data Communications
  Equipment

Data Communications Services

Data Management

Data Services

Data Systems

Deadlines

Design

Desktop Publishing

Digital Music Service

Direct Mail

DSL Products

Editing

Editorial Changes

Editorial Committee

Editorial Direction

Educational Programs

Electronic Telecommunications
  Test Equipment

E-mail Systems

Facsimile Systems

Fact Checking

Federal Agencies

Fiber-Optics

Films

Formatting

Frame Relay

Freelance Projects

Fundraising

Galleys

General Interest Topics

General Trade Reference Titles

Government Network Solutions

Grammar

Grant Proposals

HDTV

Health Care Communications
  Systems

High-Bit-Rate Digital Subscriber
  Line (HDSL)

High-Speed Data

Historical Articles

Independent Telephone
  Operating Companies

In-depth Features

Industrial Films

Institutional

Integrated Microwave Antenna
Subassemblies
Interconnect Carriers
International Newsletter
Internet
Internet Access
Internet Equipment
Interview
LAN Internetworking
Layout
Ledger
Lighting and Broadcasting
System
List Building
Local and National Affiliates
Locator Systems
Low-Radar Cross-Section
Manuscripts
Marketing
Marketing Proposals
Media Lists
Media Relations
Media Tours
Medical Journal
Monograph
Monthly Newspaper
Multimedia Group
Negotiated Contracts
Network and Data Services
Network Architectures
Network Operations

Network-Affiliated
News
News Briefs
News Casting
Newscasts
Newsletters
News Media
Newspapers
On-Air
Order Filling
Page Maker
Pamphlets
Paste-Up/Mechanicals
People Skills
Periodical Publishing
Planning and Forecasting
Packages
Poetry
Press Kits
Press Releases
Printers
Private Communications
Networks
Private Network Managers
Problem Analysis
Production
Production Details
Program Hosting
Promotions
Proofread
Props

Prototype

Public Carrier Providers

Public Relations

Public Service Announcements

Publication

Publication Process

Publicity

Publicity Files

Publishing Process

Radio Broadcasting

Record Maintenance

Recruitment Experience

References

Reporting Software

Reports

Reproduction

Research Findings

Research Papers

Research Papers and Reports

Residential Local and Long
    Distance Telephone Services

Review

Satellites

Schedules

Scholars

Scripts

Signal Reconnaissance
    Equipment

Skin

Social and Political Issues

Specialized Publications

Speeches

Stage Design

Standards and Procedures

Story Development

Story Ideas

Style Criteria

Subscribers

Subscription Orders

Subscriptions

Surface Flaws

Surveys

Switched Multimegabit Data
    Service

Tape Recording

Technical/Engineering

Telecommunications Signals

Telephone Equipment

Telephone Systems

TelePrompter

Television

Television Commercials

Text

Textbooks

Touch-Tone Telephone

Trade Magazines

Trade Newspaper

Trends

Updates

Video and Voice Applications

Videoconferencing

Voice Messaging

Voice Systems	Wireless Access Network
Voicemail	Wireless Service Plans
Voice-Processing	Word Process
Volunteer	Work Flow Systems
Wardrobe Arrangements	Writing
Wide Area Network (WAN)	

COMMONLY USED ACTION VERBS:

Acted	Generated	Proofread
Administered	Identified	Publicized
Aided	Implemented	Received
Assisted	Interviewed	Recommended
Conducted	Managed	Reported
Controlled	Operated	Researched
Coordinated	Ordered	Resolved
Created	Organized	Scheduled
Developed	Oversaw	Served
Directed	Performed	Solicited
Drafted	Planned	Supervised
Edited	Produced	Typed
Evaluated	Promoted	Wrote

ACTION VERBS AND BUZZ WORDS USED IN CONTEXT:

- *Proofread* archaeological *monographs* and museum *catalogues*.

- *Edited* and *typed grant proposals*, *research papers*, and *reports*.

- *Researched* and *wrote* items for *annual fact books* and their weekly supplemental *updates* covering the *communications* industry.

- *Reported* and *wrote* *articles* and *columns* for twice-monthly *newspaper* for the *arts and entertainment* industry.

- *Supervised* the *design* and *production* of titles for two *continuity programs*.

- *Acted* as liaison for *Marketing Director, Editor,* and *advertisers*.

- *Edited* three medical *textbooks*.

- *Wrote campaign letters; ordered* all campaign materials; staffed Campaign Advisory Committee; *coordinated* and *directed* chapter-wide meetings; *conducted* staff meetings.

- *Drafted press releases* and *speeches*.

- *Researched* and *generated story ideas*.

- *Assisted* in the *production* of *industrial films, business presentations, videotaping* of plays, fashion shows, etc.

CHAPTER TEN

COMPUTERS AND MATHEMATICS

FOR POSITIONS IN THE COM-
puter industry, buzz words are highly technical
and change fairly rapidly. Effective buzz words highlight
experience with defining, analyzing, and resolving business
problems and utilizing knowledge of computer systems to
examine problems and design solutions. Important skills
and experience include planning new computer systems or
devising ways to apply existing systems to operations that
are still done manually.

Resumes for positions in mathematics should spotlight activities ranging from the creation of new theories and techniques to the translation of economic, scientific, engineering, and managerial problems into mathematical terms.

COMMON POSITIONS INCLUDE:

Applications Programmer	Developmental Engineer
Computer Operations Supervisor	Director of Information Services
Computer Operator	Hardware Engineer
Computer Technician	Information Analyst

LAN Administrator
Manager of Network
    Administration
MIS Manager
Operations Analyst
Product Support Manager
Programming Subcontractor

Project Manager
Statistician
Systems Analyst
Systems Engineer
Systems Programmer
Technical Engineer

RESUME BUZZ WORDS:

Accounts Payable
Accounts Receivable
Administrative Tasks
Algorithms
Alternative Concept
    Development
Applications
Architecture
Architecture Requirements and
    Capabilities
Backup and Multiplatform
    Connectivity Systems
Batch System
Billing Systems
Bookkeeping
Bugs
Business Problems
Business Re-Engineering
C++
Client Database
Client Support Services
Client/Server Technology

CMS-2
COBOL Programming
Coding
Communications Technology
Computer Information Systems
Computer Interface Circuitry
Computer Program Requirements
Computer Programming
    Languages
Computer Reselling
Computer Science
Computer Software
Computer Systems
Conversion Products
Customer Needs
Customer Requirements
Customer Service System
    Consulting
Data Acquisition
Data Communication Systems
Data Communications
Data Entry

Data Migration

Data Processing

Data System Design and
    Implementation

Database Management

Database Repair/Troubleshooting

Database Systems

Deadlines

Design and Implementation

Developmental Math

Device Driver

Differential Equations

Digital Audio and Video Tools

Disk System

Documentation

DOD Telecommunications
    Technology, Architecture,
    Policy and Standards

DOS Batch Files

Drivers

Dynamical Systems Analysis

Electronic Components

Engineering Projects

Engineering Solutions

Failure and Analysis Reports

Fault Tolerant Signal Generation
    Software

File Structure

Financial Reporting Systems

Fixed Storage Space

Flowcharts

Hardware Products

Host Users

Information Architecture

Instructions and Guidelines

Integration

Internet Sales Systems

IT Planning

LAN Management

Large-Scale Networking
    Environments

Logical/Manageable Components

Mainframe Production
    Environment

Management and Technology
    Consulting

Manufacturing Efficiency

Manufacturing Test Systems

Membership Records

Memory Upgrades

Microcomputer

Mini Computers

MIS

Monitor Networks

Multiuser Database

Multivariable Calculus

Network-Based Applications

Network Configuration

Network Installation

Network Interface Cards

Network Management

Network Tools

Networking Solutions

Non-Compliant Issues

Online Message System

Open Systems

Open Systems Migration

Operating Efficiencies

Operating Systems

Operational Procedures

Optical Disks

Parallel Architectures

PC Products

PC Software

Performance Standards

Peripheral Manufacturers

Preproduction Testing

Process Control

Process Time

Product Demos

Product Presentations

Products and Components

Programming Skills

Project Cost Effectiveness

Prototype

Real-Time Computer Programs

Real-Time Embedded Software
    Design

Real-Time Interactive Visual
    Communications

Real-Time Simulation

Record Compilation

Reliability

Reporting Systems

SAS Programming

Server Machines

SGI Workstation

Shared Storage Systems

Software

Software Design

Software Development

Software Guide

Software Implementation

Software Testing

Software Upgrades

Source Code

Specifications

Statistical Knowledge

Strategic Planning

Subassemblies

System and Subsystem Interface

System Design Engineering

System Enhancements

System Safety

System Testing

Systems Configuration

Systems Engineering

Systems Test and Integration

T1 Connection

Technical Directions

Technical Notes

Technical Reports

Technical Solutions

Technology Integration

Terminal Servers	Video Images
Test Data	Visual Basic
Test Networks	Visual Programming Languages
Test Plan	Voice Communications
Test Procedures	VxWorks
Test Software/Hardware	Warehouse Development Tools
Troubleshooting	Whitepapers
Uninterrupted Transmissions	Windows
UNIX Market	Workstation Configuration
User Manuals	Workstation Maintenance
Utilities	Workstations
Video Communications	

COMMONLY USED ACTION VERBS:

Adapted	Formulated	Provided
Analyzed	Functioned	Published
Assisted	Identified	Researched
Calculated	Implemented	Resolved
Contributed	Installed	Scrutinized
Controlled	Instituted	Suggested
Correlated	Led	Supplied
Created	Maintained	Supported
Defined	Managed	Translated
Designed	Monitored	Updated
Developed	Performed	Upgraded
Directed	Presented	Wrote
Engineered	Processed	
Evaluated	Programmed	

ACTION VERBS AND BUZZ WORDS USED IN CONTEXT:

• *Designed* *network-based* *applications* for manufacturing *process control* and *test data* collection, improving product quality and manufacturing efficiency.

• *Designed* and *maintained* *computer-based* electronic *test hardware.*

• *Developed* *online message system* for members of the *programming* group.

• *Supported* existing *clients* and *resolved* critical issues/problems in a timely fashion.

• *Maintained* and *supported* the existing *COBOL mainframe online* and *batch systems.*

• *Researched* and *identified* modern replacement *hardware architecture* for existing *real-time simulation.*

• *Researched*, *identified*, and *developed* a *high-speed data communication system* connecting an *Intel Hypercube* and *Sun Sparc Workstation.*

• *Managed* large *data migration* effort.

• *Assisted* sales force in technical presentations for prospective clients.

• *Reduced* *process time* and purchasing errors by developing an *online program,* allowing the purchasing department to track the status of all invoices.

Chapter Eleven

Education and Library Sciences

EDUCATION BUZZ WORDS DISplay a familiarity with child development, kindergarten and elementary school education (including math, language, science, and social studies), private and public preschools, elementary schools, middle and secondary schools, colleges and universities, as well as tutorial operations. Library science buzz words highlight experience related to the collection and cataloging of library materials and direct information programs for the public.

Common Positions Include:

Archivist	Foreign Language Teacher
Art Instructor	Guidance Counselor
Assistant Dean of Students	Head Teacher
Coach	High School Teacher
College Professor	Kindergarten Teacher
Computer Teacher	Librarian
Daycare Worker	Library Technician
Developmental Educator	Middle School Teacher
Elementary School Teacher	Music Teacher
ESL Teacher	Nanny

Physical Education Teacher

Preschool Teacher

Principal

School Psychologist

Special Needs Educator

Teacher Aide

Tutor

Vocational Counselor

RESUME BUZZ WORDS:

Absent

Academic Development

Academic Schedule

Accountability

Accreditation

Administrative Problems

Advertising

Aesthetics

After-School Programs

Age Appropriate

Ages 8–12

ALA Filing Rules

Alertness and Coordination

Algebra I & II

Algorithm

Alumni Relations

Appreciation

Art

Artistic Skills

Audiovisual

Authentic Assessment

Author

AV Equipment

Balanced Reading

Basic Academic Skills

Behavioral Problems

Behavioral Strategies

Bibliographic Data

Bibliographies

Block Scheduling

Books

Bookstore Operations

Brain-Based Learning

Budget Planning

Building Self-Esteem

Bus Stops

Business Math

Card Catalog

Cataloging

Certification

Chair Meetings

Charter Schools

Child Development

Child-Centered Teaching

Chronically/Terminally Ill
    Children

Circulation Desk

Class Trips

Classroom Safety

Classroom Supervision

Classrooms

Coach

Cognitive Development

Cognitive Skills

Collaboration Skills

Collaborative Projects

College Archives

College-Level Courses

Committees

Computer Curriculum

Computer Lab

Computers for Classroom
    Management

Consensus

Content Areas

Copyright Policies

Course Descriptions

Crafts Instruction

Creative Expression

Creativity

Critical Thinking

Cultural and Recreational
    Activities

Curricula Methods

Curriculum

Curriculum Development

Curriculum Plans

Daily Lesson Plans

Daily Operations

Day Camp

Debater

Decode

Department of Education

Department of Social Services
    (DSS)

Department of Youth Services
    (DYS)

Departmental Text

Detention

Development of Initiative and
    Self-Reliance

Dexterity

Direct Mail

Direction

Disabled Students

Discovery Learning

Donor Gifts

Drilling

Dues

Education

Education Expeditions

Education Institutions

Education Plans

Education Reform

Education Reinforcement

Educational and Psychological
    Testing

Educational and Recreational
    Activities

Educational Committees

Educational Requirements

Elementary Education

Elementary School

Emotional Methods

Emotionally Disturbed Class

English

Environmental Simulation

Evaluation

Exercises

Faculty and Staff Counsel

Food Service Management

Fund Raising

Geometry

Grades 9–12

Grades K–8

Grades/Marks

Group Counseling

Group Presentation

Group Study

Guidance Counselor

Half-Time

Handbook

Handicaps

High School

Higher-Order Thinking

History

Honors

Index Tools

Indexes

Individual IEP's

Individual Lesson Plans

Individualized Treatment/
    Education Plans

Infant Care

Intellectual Methods

Interpreter/Translator

Journals

Junior High

Language

Language Arts

Language/Learning Disabilities

Leadership Training

Learning Aids

Learning Disability Class

Learning Through Play

Balanced Development of
    Children

Lectures/Seminars

Letter Sounds

Library Services

Life and Career Skills

Lifelong Learning

Literacy and Numeracy Skills

Mass Media Communications

Mathematics

Media Releases

Microfiche

Microfilm

Monograph Collection

Montessori Method

Multicultural Populations

Multiculturalism

Multioffice Communication

Multiple Intelligences

Museum Trips

Music Lessons

Negotiator

New Book Orders

Newsprint Publications

NLM Classification System

Nonprofit Service Organization

Numerical Ability

Observation Skills

One-to-One Instruction

On-Site Visitation

Oral Language Skills

Orientation Programs

Outcome-Based Education

Outings

Parent Involvement Committee

Parent Relations

Parent Teacher Association (PTA)

Parent-Teacher Conferences

Peer Tutoring

Performance Standards

Periodicals

Personal Care and Play

Phonics

Photo Indexing

Photocopy

Photocopy Policies

Physical Development

Physical Skills

Physical Therapy

Portfolio Assessment

Positive Behavior Modification
   Techniques

Pre-Calculus

Preparation

Preschool/Daycare Setting

Press Releases

Private School

Procedures

Program Coordination

Progress Reports

Project Approach

PTSA

Public Relations

Public School

Public Service

Public Speaking

Publishing

Pupil-Led Play

Reading

Reconstitution

Recreational Activities

Recruiting

Reference and Search Files

Reference Questions

Reference Services

Religion

Remedial Math

Remedial Reading

Research

Residence Halls

Retrospective Conversion

Role Model

Rote Learning

SAT Preparation

Scholarships

School Administration

School Board

School Policies

School Year

Science

Secondary School

Secretary of Education

Severe Emotional Disabilities
  Classroom

Sign Language

Social Studies

Special Education

Speech Pathology

Spelling

Staff Meetings

State Standards

State-Certified

Statistics

Student Accomplishments

Student Activities

Student Affairs Calendar

Student Assessment

Student Athletes

Student Evaluation

Student Groups

Student Performance

Student Relations

Substitute

Success-Oriented Group

Summer School

Superintendent

Superintendent of Public
  Instruction

Systems

Tardy

Teacher Dues

Teacher Evaluation

Teacher Recruitment

Teacher Union

Teacher-In-Service Training

Teaching Aids

Teaching Methods

Teaching Skills

Teaching to the Test

Teaching/Training

Terminals

Textbooks

Therapeutic Group Services

Traditional Teaching Mode

Training

Trigonometry

Troubleshooting Skills

University

University Students

Vocational Counseling

Vocational Interest

Voucher

Weekly Meetings

Whole Child Development   Workshops

Whole Language   Writing

COMMONLY USED ACTION VERBS:

Administered	Directed	Purchased
Aided	Ensured	Recorded
Arranged	Facilitated	Recruited
Articulated	Generated	Researched
Assisted	Handled	Reviewed
Assumed	Hired	Scouted
Budgeted	Initiated	Served
Cataloged	Instructed	Supervised
Chaired	Interviewed	Taught
Compiled	Managed	Trained
Computerized	Organized	Transferred
Conducted	Participated	Tutored
Coordinated	Performed	Worked
Created	Planned	Wrote
Designed	Prepared	
Developed	Provided	

ACTION VERBS AND BUZZ WORDS USED IN CONTEXT:

• *Handled* daily operations of college *archives*, including *cataloging, photo indexing,* and *reference services.*

• *Tutored* individuals in *reading, math,* and *oral language skills.*

• *Coordinated* the preparation and publishing of *student affairs calendar* and *advertising/press releases.*

- *Developed* a comprehensive *student activities program* focusing on development of *student's leadership skills*.

- *Conducted* *college-level courses* in *business* and *legal studies* to *university students* and *served* as *academic advisor* for *students*.

- *Purchased* and *sold* all required *textbooks* for independent *private school*.

- *Assumed* full responsibility for the set of systems, procedures, and direction of the *alumni annual fund*.

- *Taught* English to a senior Japanese *student* concentrating on special *grammar* and compositional needs.

- *Planned* *curricula* for *after-school programs* geared toward *kindergarteners* through *third graders*.

- *Provided* assessment, *counseling*, and *therapeutic group services* to parents without partners and to children of divorce.

Chapter Twelve

Engineering

BUZZ WORDS FROM THE VARious fields of engineering demonstrate experience with the theories and principles of science and mathematics and with designing machinery, products, systems, and processes for efficient and economical performance. This includes designing industrial machinery and equipment for manufacturing goods, defense systems, and weapons for the armed forces. Other important skills and experience include planning and supervising the construction of buildings, highways, and rapid transit systems; and designing and developing consumer products and systems for control and automation of manufacturing, business, and management processes.

Common Positions Include:

Aerospace Engineer	Electronics Engineer
Ceramic Engineer	Engineering Consultant
Chemical Engineer	Environmental Engineer
Civil Engineer	Facilities Engineer
Electrical Engineer	Field Engineer

Industrial Engineer

Manufacturing Engineer

Marine Engineer

Mechanical Engineer

Nuclear Engineer

Petroleum Engineer

Plastics Engineer

Product Engineer

RESUME BUZZ WORDS:

3D Modeling

Acoustic Testing

Aerodynamics

Allocation

Analog Electronics

Architecture Enhancements

Assembly Design

Assembly Modification

Bid and Cost Plus Work

Bid Sheets

Bidder Lists

Board of Safety Standards

Buildings

C Programming

C4 Navigation and
    Intelligence

Cable Products

Capital Equipment

Ceramic Capacitors

Chemical Engineering

Chemistry

Circuitry

Civil Engineering

Commercial Projects

Competitive Analysis

Complex Electromechanical
    Systems

Component Evaluation

Components and Assemblies

Compression Tests

Computer Product Design

Computer Programming

Computer Software Packages

Computer-based Transducers
    and Loudspeaker System
    Measurement

Conceptualization

Conflicts Resolution

Consistency and Compatibility

Construction Coordination

Construction Estimates

Construction Industries

Contract Engineering

Cost Reduction

Creep Tests

Customized Security

Data Collection and Analysis

Data Performance Characteristics

Design and Construction of RF
    Equipment

Design Methodologies
Design Verification Testing
Detailed Models
Development Environment
Digital Electronics
Documentation
Dynamic Systems
Economical Solution
Efficiency Control
Electrical Analysis
Electrical Design
Electrical Engineering
Electronic Design
Electronic Equipment
Electrostatic Discharge
Emissions Testing
Engineering Estimates
Engineering Field Supervision
Engineering Management
Environmental Engineering
Environmental Problems
Environmental Regulations
Environmental Testing
Equipment Maintenance
Exploration of Mines
Fabrication Methodologies
Facilities
Facilities Engineering
Facilities Inspections
Flow Patterns
Fluid Compression

Fluid Mechanics
Fluid Systems
Functional Flows
Functionality
Geological Formations
Global Marketing
Government Markets
Hardware Evaluation
High-Density Surface Mount
     Printed Circuit/Wiring
     Board (PWB)
High-Speed Applications
High-Temperature Environments
Highways
Hydraulic Systems
Hydrologic Surveys
Industrial Engineering
Industrial Projects
Information-Based Systems
Injection Molding Design
Inorganic Chemistry
Integrated Solutions and Services
Integrated Systems
Inter-Disciplinary Requirements
Internal Controls
Justification Studies
Land Surveying Services
Line Balancing
Load Monitors
Logical Performance
     Characteristics

Logistics

Machinery

Machinery Maintenance

Maintenance Documentation

Management Processes

Manufacturing

Manufacturing Problem
    Resolution

Manufacturing Processes

Marine Engineering

Master Specifications

Mathematical Models

Mathematics

Mechanical and Control Systems

Mechanical Design

Mechanical Design Integrity

Mechanical Engineering

Mechanism Design

Microscopic Analysis

Mission-Critical Programs

Motion Control

Mounting

Networked Systems

Networking Functionality

New Product Development
    Environment

OEM

Operations Manual

Part Tolerance

Parts Modeling

Performance Characteristics

Petroleum Accumulation

Petroleum Generation

Petroleum Migration

Phase Separation

Physical Performance
    Characteristics

Planning

Polishing

Powder and Bulk Solids
    Handling

Power Supply Test

Preproduction Engineering
    Prototypes

Preventive Maintenance
    Programs

Principles

Problem-Solving Skills

Procedures

Process and Procedure
    Development

Process and Project
    Documentation

Process Control

Process Development

Process Improvements

Process Methods

Process Sheets

Product Development

Productivity

Professional Consulting

Programmable Logic

Project Cost
Project Engineering
Project Management
Project Specifications
Project Start-Up
Prototypes
PWB Fabrication
Qualitative Analysis
Quality Assurance
Quality Assurance Tests
Quality Control
Quantitative Analysis
Radiation Monitoring Equipment
Radiological Controls
Reactor Design
Reactor Maintenance
Reconnaissance
Regulatory Compliance
Regulatory Requirements
Reliability
Reliability and Quality Assurance
Reliability Life Testing
Research and Development
    (R&D)
Safety Regulations
Scheduling
Science
Scientific Discovery
Sheet Metal Design
Space Platforms
Space Systems and Electronics

Specifications
Statistical Analysis
Statistical Process Controls
Stress Analysis
Structural Design
Subsystems
Surveillance
Susceptibility Testing
System Analysis
System Baselines
System Characterization and Test
System Dynamics
Systems Analysis
Systems Dynamics
Systems Maintenance
Technical Files
Technical Guidelines
Technical Guides
Technical Support
Technical Writing
Tensile Tests
Test Planning and Field
    Operations
Test Plans
Test Processes
Test Specimens
Testability and Verifiability of
    Requirements
Testing Policies
Testing Standards
Theories

Thermodynamics

Thermoforming Design

Timing Violations

Tooling

Top-Level System
    Architecture

Vendor and Partner Technology
    Relationships

Weight and Distribution
    Properties

Worst-Case Scenarios

Written Specifications

COMMONLY USED ACTION VERBS:

Analyzed	Inspected	Represented
Applied	Manufactured	Researched
Assembled	Modified	Reviewed
Assisted	Monitored	Revised
Conducted	Observed	Scheduled
Designed	Operated	Served
Developed	Oversaw	Supervised
Directed	Participated	Supported
Engineered	Performed	Trained
Established	Planned	Utilized
Evaluated	Prepared	Worked
Initiated	Provided	Wrote

ACTION VERBS AND BUZZ WORDS USED IN CONTEXT:

• *Applied* knowledge of *thermodynamics, reactor design, phase separation, fluid compression and expansion,* and *process control* to complete *simulation* from preliminary *coding.*

• *Provided* structural design and engineering estimates, and specifications for industrial, laboratory, commercial, and power facilities.

- *Evaluated* new *computer product designs*, solving *environmental* problems on *prototype computers*.

- *Assisted* engineers working on *load monitors*, which gauge *weight and distribution properties* on *heavy machine presses*.

- *Conducted* a variety of tests including *Tensile, Compression*, and *Creep* tests on *modeled parts*.

- *Assembled* machines from *drawing specifications, wire electrical boards, test and trace defects*.

- *Observed* and *participated* in exploration of mines surrounding Great Salt Lake.

- *Repaired generators, electrical motors*, and *mechanical systems* in shop, yard, and aboard rail units for public transport.

CHAPTER THIRTEEN

EXECUTIVE AND MANAGERIAL

EXECUTIVE AND MANAGERIAL

positions exist in all types of businesses. Chapter Two, on administrative positions, contains a number of words that are also relevant to applicants seeking to be managers in an office setting. Executive buzz words should highlight experience ranging from general supervisory duties to running an entire company. Relevant skills include management of individual departments within a larger corporate structure, motivating workers to achieve their goals as rapidly and economically as possibly, budgeting and directing projects, and evaluating company processes and methods to determine cost-effective plans.

COMMON POSITIONS INCLUDE:

Assistant Store Manager	Claims Examiner
Assistant Vice President	Controller
Branch Manager	Director of Operations
Chief Executive Officer (CEO)	District Manager
Chief Operations Officer	Executive Marketing Director
(COO)	Field Assurance Coordinator

Food Service Manager

General Manager

HMO Administrator

Hospital Administrator

Import/Export Manager

Insurance Claims Controller

Insurance Coordinator

Inventory Control Manager

Management Consultant

Manufacturing Manager

Operations Manager

Product Manager

Production Manager

Program Manager

Project Manager

Property Manager

Regional Manager

Retail Store Manager

Service Manager

Telecommunications Manager

Transportation Manager

Vending Manager

Vice President

Warehouse Manager

RESUME BUZZ WORDS:

Account Management

Account Retention

Accounting

Accounts Payable

Accounts Receivable

Administration

Administrative Detail

Advertising

Allocation

Annual Sales

Appointment Generation

Asset Base

Asset Management

Auditing

Audits

Banking Objectives

Banking Operations

Banking Transactions

Benefit Eligibility

Benefits Coordination

Bookkeeping

Branch Consolidation

Branch Management

Budget

Budget Development

Budget Planning

Budgeting

Budgets

Business Contacts

Business Development

Business Software

Business Strategies

Capability

Cash Administration

Cash Disbursement

Cash Flow

Certified Public Accountant
(CPA)

Check Processing

Claim Errors

Claims

Claims Adjustments

Claims Processing

Client Base

Client Relations

Cold Calling

Commercial Balances

Commercial Financing Enterprise

Commercial Loans

Commercial Paper Transactions

Commercial Real Estate

Commissions

Communications

Company Programs

Compatible

Competitive Analysis

Complaint Activity

Compliance

Consultation

Consulting

Contingency

Contract Management

Contractual Agreements

Contractual Modifications

Corporate Clients

Corporate Mission

Corporate Planning

Corporate Returns

Corporate Strategy

Correspondences

Cost Reports

Credit Lines

Custom and Importing
Regulations

Customer Education

Customer Relations

Customer Service

Data Processing

Database

Database Management

Day-to-Day Operations

Direct Mail

Direct Response Agencies

Domestic Letters of Credit

Efficient Operations

Employee Morale

Employee Training

Equipment

Evaluation

Expense Control

Expenses

Facilities

Facility Coordination

Fiduciary Income

Finance

Financial Controls

Financial Management

Financial Reports

Financial Statements

Financial Transactions

Franchise Management

General Ledgers

Hardware

High-Dollar Contracts

Hiring

Import/Export Shipments

Incremental

Individual Returns

Insurance

International Letters of Credit

Inventory

Inventory Control

Invoices

Lead Development

Leasing

Lending

Logistics

Long Term Goals

Loss Prevention

Maintenance

Major Accounts

Management

Manpower

Marketing

Marketing Activities

Markets

Merchandising

Mobility

Motivation

Negotiation

New Business Development

New Products

Objectives

Operational Objectives

Operations

Outside Sales and Support Staff

P&L Management

Payables

Payroll

Personnel Management

Personnel Relations

Policies and Procedures

Product Awareness

Profit Loss

Profit Margin

Progressive Organization

Projection

Promotions

Property Management

Prospects

Provider/Client Communication

Public Relations

Purchasing Process

Purchasing Systems

Quality Control

Receivables

Records

Referrals

Regulatory Requirements

Relationship Management

Reorganization

Reports

Restaurants

Retail Banking

Retail Sales

Revenue

Revenue Development

Sales Experience

Sales Expertise

Sales Objectives

Sales Presentations

Sales Support

Sales Techniques

Scenarios

Scheduling

Service Contracts

Service Operations

Small Business

Staff Supervision

Statistics

Store Operations

Supervision

Supervisory Experience

Tax Issues

Team Management

Technical Support

Third-Generation

Time-Phase

Training

Transitional

Troubleshooting

Yearly Transactions

COMMONLY USED ACTION VERBS:

Administered	Converted	Generated
Analyzed	Coordinated	Handled
Appointed	Decided	Headed
Approved	Delegated	Hired
Assigned	Developed	Hosted
Attained	Directed	Improved
Authorized	Eliminated	Incorporated
Chaired	Emphasized	Increased
Considered	Enforced	Initiated
Consolidated	Enhanced	Inspected
Contracted	Established	Instituted
Controlled	Executed	Led

Managed	Planned	Scheduled
Merged	Presided	Secured
Motivated	Prioritized	Selected
Navigated	Produced	Streamlined
Obtained	Recommended	Strengthened
Organized	Reorganized	Supervised
Originated	Replaced	Synchronized
Overhauled	Restored	Systematized
Oversaw	Reviewed	Terminated

ACTION VERBS AND BUZZ WORDS USED IN CONTEXT:

• *Obtained* new *accounts* to replace lost business and maintain *profitability.*

• *Utilized sales expertise* and *account management* to develop 80%-new *client base* and maintain *profit margins.*

• *Administered* and *directed marketing* activities of *banking operations.*

• *Organized* and *planned* actions impacting on various *sectors* of bank's *markets.*

• *Worked* with other *internal divisions* and *outside agencies* to develop plans that supported division's activities.

• *Planned* and *supervised training activities.*

• *Organized* a smoothly functioning *administration* and *operational division.*

• *Maintained* detailed knowledge of all aspects to include *maintenance, logistics,* and *communications.*

• *Trained* and *supervised* three claims *adjusters.*

CHAPTER FOURTEEN

FOOD AND BEVERAGES/AGRICULTURE

INDUSTRY BUZZ WORDS FOR these fields highlight experience with growing, processing, packaging, shipping, receiving, storing, preparing, and selling consumable products. This includes farming (whether it be animal, fruit, or vegetable); transport and delivery of products between farms, processing plants, and vendors; scientific research and development of products to ensure quality and safety of foods; and export and sale, both foreign and domestic.

COMMON POSITIONS INCLUDE:

Cattle Consultant

Chemist

Cost Accounting Supervisor

Customer Marketing Manager

Engineer

Food Analyst

Food Safety/Sanitation
     Worker

Food Scientist

Marketing Manager

Model Market Sales Associate

Plant Manager

Principal Flavor Scientist

Production Supervisor

Project Engineer

Project Manager

Sales Manager

Senior Brand Manager

Vending Territory Manager

RESUME BUZZ WORDS:

Advanced Breeding
Advertising Claims
Agricultural
Agricultural Chemicals
Agricultural Commodities
Agricultural Products
Agricultural Trade Association
Animal Feed Ingredients
Animal Oils
Baby Food
Baked Products
Baking Breads
Basic Ingredients
Beef
Beer
Beer Brands
Beer, Wine, and Spirits
    Distributor
Beverage Vending Company
Beverages
Biotechniques
Bottled Water
Bottling Facility
Brands
Brewing
Business Efforts
Cabernet Sauvignon
Cakes
Candy

Canned Beans
Canned Fruits and Vegetables
Canned Meat Products
Canola
Cans
Cash Advances
Cattle Feeding Procedures
Cereals
Chardonnay
Cheese
Chemical Dispensing Equipment
Citrus Growing and Processing
    Firm
Coin-Operated Vending
    Machines
Commercial Soups
Commodities
Commodity Trading
Competitive Prices
Competitively Priced
Condiments
Confections
Consumers
Convenience Food
Cookies
Cooking Oil
Corn
Corn Refining Process
Corrugating

Genetically Engineered Plants

Government Regulations

Grain Merchandising

Grain-Based Foods

Grains

Greenhouse

Groceries

Growers

Ham

Handling

Harvesting

Herbs

High-Fructose Corn Syrup

High-Quality

Horticulture

Hybrids

Ice Cream Manufacturer

Imports

Incremental Break Boxes

Industrial-Grade Starches

Ingredients

Institutions

Inventory Management

Irrigation

Juices

Ketchup

Labels

Lamb

Livestock Marketing

Livestock Production

Livestock Quality

Local Vineyards

Luncheon Meats

Major Producer

Major Trader

Malt Beverages

Manufacturer

Manufacturing

Margarine

Market

Market Conditions

Meat Products

Merchandising

Military Markets

Milk

Minerals

Mines

Nationally Distributed Food
    Products

Natural Ingredients

Nonagricultural

Nutritional Products

Oilseeds

Order Placement

Order Selection

Packaged Food Companies

Packaging

Pasta Products

Pasta Sauces

Pest Control

Pet Food

Pharmaceutical

Phosphates

Pickles

Pinot Noir

Plant Breeding

Plant Products

Planting

Pork

Portion Control

Potash

Premium Line

Premium White and Red Varietal
Table Wines

Premium Wines

Prepared Feeds

Processed Consumables

Procurement

Product Specifications

Protein Powders

Proteins

Public Stockyards

Pudding

Purchasing

Quality Control

Quality Raw Materials

Quick-Service Restaurants

Raising Livestock

Ready-To-Eat Cereals

Recognized Brand Names

Reconditioning

Refrigerated

Rent

Repackaging

Replenishment

Restaurants

Retail Food Markets

Retail Food Stores

Retail Locations

Rice

Risk Management

Rolls

Salad Dressings

Salt Products

Sauces

Sauvignon Blanc

Seafood

Seasoning Blends

Seasoning Mixes

Seasonings

Seed

Seed Varieties

Smoked Salmon Ravioli

Snack Foods

Soft Drinks

Sour Cream

Soy Flour

Soy Isolates

Soy Milk

Soy Protein

Soybeans

Spaghetti Sauces

Specialty Food Company

Specialty Food Items

Specialty Ingredient	Veal
Spices	Vegetable Oil Refinement
Sports Beverages	Vegetable Oils
Starches	Vegetable Products
Sterility Control	Vegetables
Storing	Vendors
Strain Management	Vitamin C
Sweeteners	Vitamin E
Temperature Controlled	Vitamins
Tomato Sauces	Wheat
Tomato-Based Products	Wholesale Food Distributors
Transporting	Wholesale Outlets
Tryptophan	Wholesaler
TVP	Yogurt

COMMONLY USED ACTION VERBS:

Acquired	Harvested	Planted
Bred	Imported	Produced
Controlled	Improved	Researched
Developed	Managed	Sold
Displayed	Manufactured	Supplied
Distributed	Marketed	Worked
Ensured	Organized	
Exported	Oversaw	

ACTION VERBS AND BUZZ WORDS USED IN CONTEXT:

• *Organized delivery* of *convenience foods* to major *vendors* and *supermarket chains*.

• *Managed order placement*, *transporting*, *receiving* and *storing* of *soy products* for *wholesale outlets*.

- *Developed* improved *market conditions* for local *vineyards* and *wineries*.

- *Displayed* knowledge of *government regulations* and *product specifications* for *quality control* purposes.

- *Worked* with *food production tests* for such foods as *luncheon meats*, *vegetable oils* and *canned fruit products*.

- *Exported specialty food items* to worldwide *distributors* of *convenience foods*.

- *Researched* the effects of *temperature control* on *vitamins*, *starches*, *proteins*, and *minerals* during *food processing*.

- *Marketed pet food products* to domestic buyers.

- *Ensured cattle feeding* procedures ran smoothly and efficiently during crucial *cattle growth* stages.

- *Oversaw* daily operations of *greenhouse*, including *planting*, *pest control*, *plant breeding*, and *harvesting*.

CHAPTER FIFTEEN

GOVERNMENT

FOR THOSE INTERESTED IN positions in politics and government, buzz words highlight experience in executive, legislative, judicial, or general government agencies as well as with public agencies, such as firefighting, military, police work, or the United States Postal Service. This includes researching and evaluating military materials; cleaning, maintenance, and general service for public works; participating in political campaigns by networking, fundraising, or organizing; and working to control narcotic and dangerous drug use through prevention and law enforcement. It also includes mail pickup and delivery experience, public relations and press work, and public outreach activities.

COMMON POSITIONS INCLUDE:

Advocacy Program Coordinator	Community Development Technician
Archives Specialist	Community Planner
Automation Clerk	Contract Specialist
Claims Assistant	Education Technician

Firefighter

General Engineer

General Health Scientist

Health Inspector

Laborer

Law Clerk

Loan Specialist

Mail Carrier

Nuclear Medicine Technologist

Office Assistant

Outdoor Recreation Planner

Park Ranger

Public Defender

Purchasing Agent

Recreation Specialist

Transportation Security Specialist

Utility Systems Repairer

Operator

Resume Buzz Words:

Administration

Administrative Offices

Administrative Services

Advanced Development Programs

Agency

Agency Management

Agricultural Production

Agriculture

Air and Water Pollution

Air Quality

Annex Building

Area-Wide Governmental
Organization

Assistance Services

Bank Holding Companies

Borrowing Transactions

Briefing Reports

Broadly Based Exploratory
Programs

Building Activities

Bureau

Business Administration

Business Interests

Business Relationship

Central Headquarters

Central Management Agencies

Chamber of Commerce

Citizens

City Council Offices

City Departments

City Highways

City Manager

City Transportation
Department

Classification Compliance Audits

Coastal Waters

Committee

Community Service Jobs

Complete Range of Mail Pickup
and Delivery Services

Fire Prevention
Fish and Wildlife
Food Protection Program
Food Stamps
Foreign Intelligence
Functional Divisions
Funding
General Services
Generating Electricity
Government Assistance
Government Offices
Government Organization
Government Program
   Applications
Government Registration
   Activities
Governmental Organization
Government-Owned Facilities
Government-Run
Governor
Grant
Guidelines
Health and Human Services
   Facility
Highway Maintenance
Human Health Protection
Impact of Trade
Import
Inadequate Housing
Income Distribution
Income Tax Returns

Independent Auditor
Information Services
Information Technology
In-House Research
Institutional Issues
International Agency
International Aid
International Companies
International Lending Agency
International Trade
Issuance of Licenses
Job Market
Job Placement
Jobseekers
Justice
Labor Unions
Land Use
Law
Law Enforcement Services
Legal Cases
Legal Determinations
Legal Services
Legislative Branch
Legislative Requests
Legislators
Lending to Third World Nations
Local Businesses
Local Government Agency
Local Office
Long-term Economic Growth
Macroeconomics

Maintenance and Improvement

Mandate

Manufacturing Quotas

Mayor's Office

Medicaid Services

Medical Devices

Medical Emergencies

Medico-Public Health
   Laboratory

Metro

Metropolitan Development

Missions

Monetary Policy

Monetary Theory

Multidisciplinary Support

National Cemeteries

National Headquarters

National Health Programs

National Law Enforcement
   Agency

National Parks

Nationwide Health Care
   Programs

Natural Resources

Nature and Wildlife Preservation

Naval Warfare Centers

Navy Needs

Nonprofit

Nuclear Materials

Nuclear Power

Objective Trade Expertise

Operations

Organization Analysis

Passport Acceptance

Patent

Patrols

Physical Sciences

Police Department

Policies

Political and Legislative Support
   Functions

Political Economy

Productivity of Natural
   Resources

Public Buildings

Public Expenditure

Public Finance

Public Order

Public Use

Public Works

Purify City Water

Quality Health Care

Quality of the Environment

Radiation Emitting Products

Recreation Areas

Rectifying Disputes

Recycling Services

Reducing Manufacturing Costs

Regional Offices

Regional Planning Agency

Regional Problems

Regional Training Institutes

Regulation of Companies

Regulatory Agency

Regulatory Commission

Renewable Energy

Repair Services

Republican Party

Roads and Highways

Safe Living Conditions

Sale of Consumer Products

Securities Market

Security Documents

Security Products

Seminars

Senior Services

Significant Economic Changes

Small Business

Snow Plowing

Space Systems Technology

Special Investigations

Standards

State Entities

State Government

State Parks and Reservations

State Representation

State Tax Information

State-Run Agencies and Universities

Statewide Financial and Compliance Audits

Statistical Material

Statistical Methodologies

Statutory Filings

Street Repairs

Tax Forms

Tax Publications

Trade Actions

Trade Association

Trade Seminars

Traffic Congestion

Transportation Planning

U.S. Industries

U.S. Paper Currency

U.S. Policy

Urban Development

Utility Companies

Volunteers

Water Supply

Welfare Office

Work Force Conditions

Workers' Compensation Claims

COMMONLY USED ACTION VERBS:

Campaigned	Investigated	Participated
Delegated	Lobbied	Practiced
Demonstrated	Managed	Processed
Dispatched	Organized	Raised

Researched	Supervised	Volunteered
Served	Supported	
Settled	Updated	

ACTION VERBS AND BUZZ WORDS USED IN CONTEXT:

- *Demonstrated* problem-solving skills and *diplomatic* capabilities in dealing with *federal labor-management relations.*

- *Campaigned* for the *Democratic Party,* focusing on significant *economic changes, recycling services, regulation of companies,* and *safe living conditions.*

- *Processed* incoming and outgoing mail for sorting and distribution; *updated postal rates* and sold stamps.

- *Managed fire prevention* activities and the protection of *citizens* in fire or *medical emergencies.*

- *Dispatched law enforcement officers* and *rescue personnel* in *emergency situations.*

- *Supervised* daily functions at *national park,* including trash pickup, water supply, repair services; *managed park headquarters.*

- *Volunteered* at center for *senior services and welfare.* Responsibilities included helping to ensure safe living conditions, tracking *Medicaid services,* and being on call for *emergency situations.*

- *Investigated* cases of *worker's compensation claims* for *public defender* and compiled *statistical material* into spreadsheets.

- *Raised* drug prevention awareness by *organizing* support functions and seminars.

- *Practiced* law as a *public defender* in *district court* for ten years, primarily handling cases concerning domestic disputes and custody battles.

Chapter Sixteen

Health and Medical

BUZZ WORDS FROM THE VITAL health and medical fields demonstrate experience with illness, working toward achieving and maintaining healthy lifestyles and helping to address and resolve related issues, such as insurance and medical claim forms. This includes working directly with patients and their families in dealing with health problems; assisting patients by providing medical advice regarding prescriptions, insurance claim forms, and related issues; and researching medical treatments and techniques.

Common Positions Include:

Cardiologist

Chiropractor

Clinical Director

Dental Assistant

Dental Hygienist

Dental Technician

Dentist

Dietary Technician

Dietician

Emergency Medical
    Technician

Fitness Instructor

Health Services Coordinator

Home Health Aide

Hospital Supervisor

Intern

Lab Technician

Medical Records Clerk

Medical Student

Medical Technologist

MRI Coordinator

Nurse

Nursing Administrator

Nursing Aide

Nursing Home Manager

Nursing Supervisor

Nutritionist

Occupational Therapist

Optician

Orthodontist

Pediatrician

Pharmacist

Pharmacy Technician

Physical Therapist

Physician's Assistant

Psychiatrist

Resident

Respiratory Therapist

Speech Pathologist

Surgeon

Veterinarian

RESUME BUZZ WORDS:

Acute and Chronic Patients

Agency Staff

AIDS

Ambulatory Services

Anatomy/Physiology

Anesthesia Operations

Angioplasty

Appointments

Behavioral Programs

Biochemistry

Blood Chemistry

Blood Draws

Bone Fractures

Budget Preparation

Budget Responsibilities

Burn Patients

Business Management Activities

Calisthenics

Cardiac Anatomy

Cardiac Catheterization

Cardiac Patients

Case Management

Childbirth

Chronic Pain

Chronically Ill

Clerical Support

Client Eligibility

Clinical Cardiology

Clinical Instruction

Clinical Operations

Communication Disorders

Community Hospitals

In-Service Consultation

Instrument Set-Ups

Insurance Companies

Intensive Aerobics

Intravenous Therapy

IV Antibiotic Therapy

Lab Procedures

Lab Results

Laboratory Operations

Lathes

Manic Depression

Massage Therapy

Medical Equipment

Medical Management

Medical Photography

Medical Records

Medical Research

Methodology

Metropolitan Hospitals

Modalities

Motivational Skills

MRI Department

Multidisciplined Practice

New Medications

Nursing Home Placement

Nursing Practice Standards

Nursing Services

Nutrients

Nutrition

Nutritional Care Plans

Order Entry

Outpatient

Parenteral and Enteral Nutrition

Pathology

Patient Care

Patient Charts

Patient Records

Patient Relations

Patient Services

Patients

Pediatric Patients

Pediatric/Emergency Medicine

Personality Disorders

Pet Food Products

Pet Nutrition

Pharmaceutical Companies

Pharmaceuticals

Pharmacology

Pharmacology and Behavioral
    Modification Methods

Physical and Psychosocial Needs

Physical Standards

Physical Therapy Standards

Policy and Procedures
    Development

Polishers

Post-Op Care

Post-Operative Care

Preliminary Diagnoses

Pre-Operative Care

Prescription Reimbursement
    Claims

Prescriptions
Primary Nursing Care
Private Practice
Psychiatric Care
Psychology
Psycho-Social Assessments
QA Monitoring
Qualitative Research
Quality Assurance
Quantitative Research
Radiology
Referring Physicians
Respiratory Therapy
Service Related Incidents
Severely Ill Patients
Side Effects
Skilled Nursing Assessment
Social Services
Specialized Nursing and Medical
    Care
Staffing Issues
State-Funded Programs
Statistical Reports

Strength and Stamina
Stretching
Stretching/Strengthening
    Exercises
Strokes
Substance Abuse
Surgical Procedures
Teaching
Therapy
Tracheotomy Care
Ultrasound
Unit Doses
Urinalysis
Ventilators
Veterinary Medicine
Vital Signs
Word Processing
Work-Related Injuries
Workshops
X-Ray Department
X-Ray Procedures
Yoga

COMMONLY USED ACTION VERBS:

Acted	Arranged	Completed
Administered	Assessed	Conducted
Advised	Assisted	Conferred
Alleviated	Assumed	Constructed
Allocated	Attended	Consulted
Analyzed	Collaborated	Coordinated

Created	Initiated	Recommended
Dealt	Instructed	Recorded
Demonstrated	Interviewed	Redesigned
Determined	Invited	Required
Developed	Led	Requisitioned
Directed	Lectured	Researched
Dispensed	Maintained	Reviewed
Distributed	Managed	Scheduled
Drafted	Monitored	Selected
Educated	Motivated	Served
Encouraged	Observed	Serviced
Ensured	Operated	Specialized
Established	Organized	Started
Evaluated	Oriented	Structured
Facilitated	Participated	Supervised
Fielded	Performed	Supported
Filled	Planned	Taught
Formed	Prepared	Trained
Functioned	Presented	Typed
Geared	Priced	Updated
Generated	Produced	Used
Handled	Provided	Utilized
Hired	Purchased	Worked
Identified	Ran	Wrote
Implemented	Received	

ACTION VERBS AND BUZZ WORDS USED IN CONTEXT:

• *Provided* spinal manipulation and *handled* necessary *muscular-skeletal* needs of *sports-injured patients.*

- *Provided* information for *insurance companies, workman's compensation,* and *third-party billing procedures.*

- *Supervised* 75 *clinical,* administrative, and staff employees.

- *Coordinated treatment* and *discharge planning.*

- *Prepared patients* for *surgical procedures*; *recorded temperature* and *blood pressure, inserted intravenous units,* and *administered sedatives.*

- *Scheduled patients* for appointments.

- *Monitored radiographs* and *administered Novocain* prior to *procedures.*

- *Assisted dentist* in *prophylactic procedures*: *provided* necessary tools, *sterilized* equipment, *comforted patients.*

- *Taught* intensive *aerobics, calisthenics,* and *stretching* to co-educational classes of up to 25 adults in all physical conditions.

- *Organized labs* for *veterinary* students and for *clinical instruction.*

- *Directed hygienic procedures* on 300 animals including *surgical* and *necropsies.*

- *Instructed* and *supervised Home Health Aides.*

- *Served* as *clinical instructor* for *physical therapy* students and *Pulmonary Clinic.*

- *Drafted physical therapy standards of care* for selected *surgical procedures.*

- *Requisitioned* all *laboratory supplies*; *participated* in conferences with *medical staff* on *patients* with special *laboratory* needs.

- *Conducted* hematology and *serology testing*, as well as *test sample photography*.

- *Operated* hematology laboratory using *haemacount machine, leitz photometer*, and *EKF machine*.

CHAPTER SEVENTEEN

HOTELS AND RESTAURANTS

IN THESE SERVICE INDUSTRIES, buzz words reflect experience and familiarity with restaurant management, food services, banquets and conventions, guest/customer service, and promotions. Other valuable skills include culinary, business/accounting, interpersonal communication, and facilities management. Many of these buzz words would also apply for many positions in the travel industry (see Chapter Twenty-Nine).

COMMON POSITIONS INCLUDE:

Baker	General Manager
Banquet Houseman	Hostess
Bell Person	Housekeeping Supervisor
Breakfast Cook	Human Resources
Busser	Coordinator
Counter Server	Lifeguard
Floor Supervisor	Line Cook
Food Service Manager	Maintenance Engineer
Front Desk Agent	Massage Therapist
Front Desk Receptionist	Mini-Bar Attendant

Pastry/Prep Cook

PBX Operator

Porter

Restaurant Manager

Room Attendant

Sous Chef

Spa Attendant

Utility Person

Waiter

Weight Room Attendant

RESUME BUZZ WORDS:

ACF (CEC) Certification

ACF Apprenticeship

Administrative

Amusement Facilities

Audio Equipment

Bakeries

Bakery and Confectionery

Banquet Activities

Banquet Equipment

Banquet/Meeting Facilities

Bar Set-Up and Breakdown

Beauty Culture

Bookkeeping

Budgeted Food Costs

Buffet and Restaurant Displays

Buffing Wheel

Burnishing Machine Tumble

Cafes

Cash Control

Cash Handling Procedures

Casual-Dining Restaurants

Catering

China, Glass and Silver Service
    Inventory

Cleanliness

Cleanup of All Banquet
    Functions

Cocktails

Company Standards

Conference Center

Cookery Craft

Coolers/Storerooms

Country Clubs

Culinary Arts

Culinary Management

Culinary School

Cultural Centers

Customer Satisfaction

Daily Quality Checks

Deluxe Hotels

Dinnerware

Dishwashing Machine

DJs

Drive-Thru Restaurants

Eating Venues

Employee Relations

Ethnic Cuisine

Excess Production

Exclusive Health Clubs

Family-Oriented Restaurants

Fast-Food Restaurants

Federal, State, Local Safety and
    Health Regulations

Fine Dining

Floor and Capacity Charts

Flow of Guests

Food and Facilities Management
    Services Company

Food and/or Beverage Orders

Food Preparation and
    Presentation

Food Preservation

Food Production Management

Food Retailing

Food Service Companies

Food Service Facilities

Food Service Handlers
    Certification

Foreign Hotel Institutions

Franchises

Fresh Products

Front Office Operation

Glassware

Global Sales

Groundskeeping

Guest Occupancy

Guest Services

HACCP Standards

Health Department Rules

Hiring

Home Science

Hospitality Management

Hotel Accounting

Hotel Management

Hotel Standards

Housekeeping

Ingredients

Integrated Facilities Management

International Hospitality

Inventory and Food Costs

JCAHO Knowledge

Kitchen

Leisure and Tourism

Leisure Attractions

Licensed House Management

Liquor and Wines

Live Entertainment

Luxury Hotel

Management Experience

Meat Blocks

Meeting Rooms

Menu

Menu Development

Menu Planning for Various
    Disease States

Nightclub Promotions

Nutritional Requirements

Nutritional Screening and
    Assessment

Online Reservations

Organizational Functions

Orientation

Outsourcing Solutions

Personality

Pizzeria

Plant Operations and
Maintenance

Plating and Presentation

Portion Sizes

Pots, Pans, and Trays

Presentation

Pre-Shift and Regularly
Scheduled Meetings

Prices

Problem-Solving Capabilities

Promotions

Proper Food Handling

Public Recreation Facilities

Quality Standards

Reception

Recruiting Efforts

Refrigerators

Reservation

Resorts

Restaurants

Roadside Lodges

Room Set-Ups

Safety Procedures

Sales Figures

Sanitation Practices

Scheduling

Server Stations

Special Packages and Promotions

Spoilage

Squirrel POS System

Staff Development

Staffing

Tables

Techniques and Standards

TIPS Certification

Tourism

Training

Trash and Garbage Removal

Travel

Vendor and Distributor Relations

Vocational Training

Weddings

Weekly and Monthly Inventories

Worktables

COMMONLY USED ACTION VERBS:

Adhered	Escorted	Maintained
Assisted	Established	Managed
Communicated	Greeted	Monitored
Ensured	Hired	Participated

| Provided | Scheduled | Trained |
| Recommended | Supervised | Worked |

ACTION VERBS AND BUZZ WORDS USED IN CONTEXT:

• *Worked* the *front desk*, *greeted guests*, *completed check in* and *check out transactions*, and answered multi-line telephone.

• *Provided* general information and *assisted guests* regarding *hotel services*.

• *Recommended* the *hotel's budget*, *marketing plans*, and *business plans* and *managed* within approved plans and objectives.

• *Hired*, *trained*, *supervised*, *scheduled*, and *participated* in activities of *chefs*, *cooks*, and other personnel involved in *preparing*, *cooking*, and *presenting food* in accordance with productivity standards, cost controls, and forecast needs.

• *Escorted arriving* and *departing guests* in a friendly and courteous manner to and from their *accommodations*.

• *Managed* the daily *production*, *preparation*, and *presentation* of all food for the *hotel's restaurant* and *room service*.

• *Monitored* and *maintained* level of cleanliness in *room storage areas*, *laundry*, *restrooms*, and *public areas*.

• *Established* and *maintained costs control systems* for *staffing linen inventories* and *cleaning supplies*.

• *Assisted* in the *management* and *oversight* of all *kitchen operations*.

CHAPTER EIGHTEEN

HUMAN RESOURCES

HUMAN RESOURCE BUZZ words display experience recruiting, interviewing, and hiring employees according to their qualifications and suitability to the organization. Additional responsibilities often include encouraging a productive company culture by effectively utilizing employee skills and fostering job satisfaction; handling employee health and pension plans; and maintaining and articulating knowledge of government regulations regarding labor and employee benefit regulations.

COMMON POSITIONS INCLUDE:

Assistant Personnel Officer

Assistant Vice President of
     Human Resources

Benefits Coordinator

Compensation Manager

Director of Human Resources

Employee Relations
     Representative

Employment Consultant

Facility Manager

Job Placement Officer

Labor Relations Specialist

Personnel Consultant

Personnel Manager

Recruiter

Training Specialist

Vice President of Human
     Resources

RESUME BUZZ WORDS:

Accounts Payable System

Accounts Receivable System

Ad Management

ADA

Administration

Affirmative Action

Background Checks

Behavioral Sciences

Benchmarking

Benefit Checks

Benefit Consulting

Benefits

Benefits Administration

Competencies

Blended Learning Solutions

Business Results

Business Value

Candidate Pool

Candidate Screening

Career Counseling

Career Development

Career Fairs

Claim Adjudication

Client Management

Coached Learning Solutions

Coaching

College Programs

Compensation and Payroll Functions

Compensation Consulting

Compensation Data

Compensation System

Confidential Personnel Records

Consultative Skills

Content Assessment

Contract Negotiations

Contracts

Corporate Communication

Corporate Learning

Corporate Performance

Corporate Philosophy

Creation of Reports and
    Correspondences

Current Trends

Customer Service

Delivery Assessment

Departmental Contacts

Departmental Expenditures

Development Initiatives

Direct Mail

EEO/AA Compliance

e-Learning

Electronic Learning Solutions

Employee Counseling

Employee Effectiveness

Employee Records

Employee Relations

Employee Relationship
    Management Solution

Payroll Database

Payroll Transmissions

Pension/Health and Welfare
Reports

People Development

Performance Development

Performance Management

Performance Measurement and
Rewards

Permanent Personnel Actions

Permanent Positions

Personnel

Personnel Policies

Placement

Portfolio assessment

Position Analysis

Potential Candidates

Pre-Screening

Pricing Information

Private Sector

Productivity

Professional Associations

Professional Development

Professional Staffing Costs

Program Delivery

Progressive Human Processes

Prospective Employees

Qualified Professionals

Real-Time Information

Recruiting Resources

Recruitment

Recruitment Sources

Reference Checks

Referrals

Regulations

Regulatory Agencies: EOHS,
OER, DPA, PERA

Reinsurance Carrier

Request For Proposals (RFP)

Resume Preparation

Retirement Consulting

Return On Investment (ROI)

Salaried Jobs

Salary Administration

Salary Reviews

Salary Surveys

Self-Directed Learning Solutions

Skills Testing

Staffing

Statistical Records

Strategic Human Resource
Planning

Team Development

Team Performance

Team-Based Environment

Telemarketing

Temporary Assignments

Termination

Time and Labor Solutions

Training

Tutoring

Unclaimed Wages

Unemployed Youth

Unemployment Insurance

Unions

Unskilled

Vacation Schedules

Vendor Selection

Visitors

Wages

Web-Based Enterprise
    Applications

Website Job Postings

Worker's Compensation

Workflow

Workplace Laws

Workplace Stress

COMMONLY USED ACTION VERBS:

Administered

Advised

Analyzed

Assign

Assisted

Conducted

Coordinated

Counsel

Delegated

Developed

Entered

Established

Evaluated

Expanded

Facilitated

Handled

Hired

Improved

Interpreted

Interviewed

Investigated

Logged

Maintained

Managed

Monitored

Motivated

Organized

Paid

Participated

Performed

Placed

Prepared

Professionalized

Recommend

Reconciled

Recruited

Reduced

Researched

Resolved

Responded

Reviewed

Revised

Screened

Served

Signed

Solved

Spearheaded

Supervised

Terminated

Trained

Updated

Verified

Action verbs and buzz words used in context:

- *Organized*, *revised*, *expanded*, and *managed* *induction program*.

- *Reconciled* all *checks* to the *unclaimed wages account*.

- *Provided* *employee relations* support and consultation to three departments.

- *Supervised* *claim adjudication*.

- *Coordinated* statewide *reclassification study*.

- *Interviewed* *employers*; *gathered* information; *determined* status in *claims cases*.

- *Prepared* daily balances; *managed* cash.

- *Established* and *maintained* contact with various civic, cultural, and community organizations.

CHAPTER NINETEEN

INSURANCE

FOR THE INSURANCE INDUSTRY, appropriate buzz words highlight experience with contracts, claims, personal injury, workman's compensation, and assets. This includes knowledge of different areas of insurance, such as fire, theft, automotive, property, business, health, and disability. Familiarity with premiums, appraisals, policies, financial planning services, and insurance sales should also be included.

COMMON POSITIONS INCLUDE:

Account Sales Executive	Claims Examiner
Actuary	Claims Legal Senior
Agency Manager	Correspondent
Analyst	Claims Professional
Appointment Clerk	Clinical Intake Specialist
Associate Agent	Consultant
Beneficiary Services	Financial and Operations
Representative	Auditor
Broker	Information Specialist
Casualty Claim Analyst	Insurance Adjuster

Insurance Agent

Insurance Manager

Insurance Sales Representative

Licensed Insurance Agent

Market Point Sales Representative

Personal Lines Account Manager

Professional Benefit Enroller

Sales Executive

Sales Specialist

Underwriter

RESUME BUZZ WORDS:

Accident

Accountability

Accounts Receivable

Act of God

Adhesion

Adjust

Adjustment

Advance

Agency

Agents

Aggregate

Aid

Amendment

Annuities

Annuity Plans

Annuity Products

Appraisal

Asset Accumulation

Asset-Based Lending/Financing

Assets

Attorneys

Audit

Auto Insurance Claims

Automobile Accident

Automobile Dealers

Automobile Insurance

Automotive

Basic Coverage

Benefits

Binding Agreement

Book Value

Borderline Risk

Branch Offices

Broad-Based Customer Group

Brokerage

Building Code

Capacity

Capital

Captive Agents

Care Plan

Carrier

Caseload

Cash Value

Casualty

Certificate

Charitable Health Care
Corporation

Charter

Claims

Claims Management Services

Class

Clause

Clients

Closing Services

Collision

Commercial and Individual
    Financial Services

Commercial Clients

Commercial Insurance

Commission

Common Law

Compensation

Consolidation

Contingency

Contract

Convention

Convergence

Conversion

Countersignature

Coverage

Covered Loss

Credit Associations

Credit Insurance

Credit Life Insurance

Credit Report

Customers

Daily Report

Damage

Deductible

Dental Care Services

Dental Insurance Firm

Dependents

Descendent

Disability Coverage

Disability Income Insurance

Earned

Emergency Coverage

Endorsement

Enterprise

Equity

Escrow

Estate

Estate Planning

Exclusion

Expense

Extended

Fee

Field

Financial and Insurance
    Operations

Financial Services Group

Firm

First Party

Flat

Gain

Geographical Location

Gross

Group Health

Group Life

Group Pension

Guiding Principle

Hazard

Health Care Delivery

Health Maintenance
Organizations (HMO)

Health Plan Coverage

High Exposure Claims

Holding Company

Homebuyers

Homeowners

Indemnity Medical

Individual Life

Inevitable Accident

Injury

Inspection

Institutional Investments

Insurance Carrier

Insurance Products

Insurance Provider

Insurance Risks

Interest Rate

Investigation

Investment

Investment Planning

Investment Planning Company

Joint Coverage

Jurisdictions

Leaseholder

Lenders

Lending Organizations

Liabilities

License

Life Insurance

Limitations

Liquidation

Loss

Loss Prevention

Major Disasters

Malpractice Insurance

Market Value

Members

Mortgage

Multiline Financial Services

Multiperil

Multiple-Line

Mutual Funds

Mutualization

Natural Death

Negligence

Net Loss

Noninsurable Risk

Nonrenewal

Offices

Outsource Vendor

Overrides

Ownership

Payee

Pension

Pension Planning Markets

Performance Reports

Permanent Insurance

Personal Automobiles

Personal Injury	Quota
Personal Insurance	Rates
Personal Lines of Insurance	Real Estate Brokers
Policies	Real Estate Transactions
Policy Cancellation	Rebate
Policy Writing	Records
Policyholders	Regional and Specialty Property
Portfolio	and Casualty Insurers
Power of Attorney	Reinsurance Intermediary
Premium Rate	Facilities
Premiums	Renewal
Prevention	Retirement Planning
Primary Coverage	Risk Management Programs
Primary Insurers	Risks
Procedures	Search and Examination Services
Product Portfolio	Securities
Professional Liability Insurance	Selling
Professional Medical Services	Services
Proof of Loss	Settlement
Property	Severity
Property and Casualty	Special Accounts
Reinsurance	Sum
Provider Reimbursement	Surety
Providers	Title Insurance

COMMONLY USED ACTION VERBS:

Computed	Evaluated	Processed
Created	Filed	Recorded
Delivered	Implemented	Sold
Developed	Interacted	Updated
Estimated	Negotiated	Worked

ACTION VERBS AND BUZZ WORDS USED IN CONTEXT:

• *Evaluated* client portfolios for *claims*; *filed* regarding *personal injury* and *negligence*.

• *Worked* as an *actuary*; *computed premiums* and *insurance risks* in conjunction with supporting team.

• *Interacted* with *customers* daily to explain *annuity plans*, *real estate transactions*, and *claims*.

• *Adjusted premium rates* for *commercial and individual financial services*; *notified* clients of *renewal periods*.

• *Updated records* regarding *policies* and *procedures* to be ready for use by *real estate brokers*.

• *Recorded* proof of loss and *delivered* reimbursement *checks*.

• *Assisted* individuals in selection of *insurance policies*. *Worked* to ensure lowest *rates* and highest *coverage* possible to fit individual needs.

• *Computed settlements* for *homeowners* after *major disasters*.

• *Implemented* employee wellness programs for *special accounts* during *renewal periods*.

• *Conducted automotive claims investigations* to determine *net loss*.

• *Worked* in *professional liability insurance* advocating the rights of *policyholders*.

CHAPTER TWENTY

LEGAL AND PROTECTIVE SERVICES

IN THESE FIELDS, BUZZ WORDS highlight experience with interpreting and enforcing the laws. This includes supporting the legal system; patrolling and inspecting property to protect against theft, vandalism, and illegal entry; and ensuring the safety and security of persons who have been arrested, are awaiting trial, or who have been convicted of a crime and sentenced to serve time in a correctional institution. It also includes maintaining order, enforcing rules and regulations, and supplementing counseling.

COMMON POSITIONS INCLUDE:

Assistant Attorney General	Law Student
Attorney	Legal Assistant
Contracts Manager	Legal Secretary
Correctional Officer	Loss Prevention Manager
Court Officer	Paralegal
Court Reporter	Patent Agent
Fire Fighter	Peer Counselor
Guard	Police Officer
Law Clerk	Police Sergeant

RESUME BUZZ WORDS:

Administrative Hearings

Administrative Support
   Services

Advisory Committees

Advisory Opinions

Alarms

Ambulance

Anti-Theft System

Appeals Court

Appellate Briefs

Appellate Litigation

Applicants

Appointments

Appropriate Parties

Arbitrators

Arraignment

Assigned Areas

Attorney Appearance Records

Attorney-Client Conferences

Bail Agreements

Bail Motions

Bankruptcy

Bankruptcy Trustees

Brief

Budgeting

Building Security

Burglar Alarms

Bylaws

Camera Surveillance System

Campaign Activities

Capital Projected Costs

Care and Protection Cases

Case Files

Case Management Project

Case Research

Cell Checks

Citations

City Property

Civil Action

Civil Litigation

Civil Motions

Civil Pleadings

Civil Probate Court

Civil Proceedings

Civil Rights

Clerical Support

Client Forms

Client Needs

Client Scheduling

Client Service Plans

Clients

Client's Suit

Co-Counsel

Codes

Collective Bargaining Issues

Commercial Accounts

Commercial Law Department

Commissions

Committee Hearings

Communication Law

Community Outreach

Community Relations

Community Resources

Complaints

Complex Litigation

Computerized Information
System

Conciliations

Conclusion of Law

Confidential Reports

Constituents

Contract Administration

Contract Law

Contractual Support

Copyright Registration and
Licensing

Corporate Acquisitions

Corporate Compliance

Corporate Data

Corporate Documents

Corporate Financing

Corporate Law

Corporate Tax Standing

Corporate Votes

Correctional Institutions

Correspondence

Cost Analysis

Cost Records

Court

Court Proceedings

Court Reporter

Court Scheduling

Court Sessions

Court Transcripts

Courthouses

Courtroom

Courtroom Activity

CPR/First Aid

Crime Deterrence

Crime Prevention

Crime Zones

Criminal Action

Criminal Arrest Citations

Criminal Cases

Criminal Investigations

Criminal Law

Criminal Motions

Criminal Proceedings

Criminal Situations

Crisis Intervention

Custody/Traffic Direction
Processes

Deadlines

Debtors

Defamation Claims

Defendants

Defense Attorney

Delegation of Tasks

Department of Corrections

Department Procedure

Departmental Goals and Direction

Deposition

Deposition Hearings

Discharge

Discharge Petitions

Discovery

Discovery Motions

Dissolution Plans

District Attorney's Office

District Court

Drafting Wills

Drafts

Elective Offices

Emergency

Emergency Situations

Emergency Transportation

Emotional Status

Energy Maintenance Program

Enlistment

Environmental Arenas

Environmental Litigation

Environmental Programs

Environmental Status

Evaluation

Evidence Information

Execution of Duties

Extensive Corporate Dealings

Facilities

Fact

False Advertising

False Claims

Final Payments

Final Settlement Statement

Financial Institutions

Financing Statements

Fingerprints

Fire Academy

Fire Fighting

Fire Prevention

Firearms

Firearms Qualified

Foot Patrols

Forensic Fire Photography

General Business Litigation

General Laws

General Patrol Responsibilities

General Practice

General Practice Law Firm

General Public

General Security Proceedings

Good Will

Government

Government Agencies

Governmental Communications

Grand Jury Testimony

Guard Forces

Guardianship

Guidance

Hearing Practice

High Crime Area

High Pressure Arenas

Hospital Transportation

Housing Area

Human Services

Immigration Case Conferences

In Custody

Incentive Programs

Incident Reports

Inmate Population

Inpatient Facilities

Inquiry Recording System

Insurance Claims

Insurance Companies

Intellectual Property Law

Interviewing of Witnesses

Investigation of Losses

Investigations

Involved Parties

Judicial Arenas

Judicial Lobbies

Justices

Juvenile Court

K-9 Handler

Labor Law

Labor Litigation

Labor Relation Issues

Larceny

Law

Law Enforcement

Law Enforcement Agencies

Law Firm

Law Office Accounts

Law Schools

Legal Counsel

Legal Opinions

Legal Research

Legislation

Legislative Bills

Legislatively Mandated Advisory
Committee

Library Research

Licensing

Liens

Liquidation

Litigation Experience

Litigation of False Advertising

Loan Documents

Lobby

Local Agencies

Long-Term Care Issues

Loss Prevention

Maintenance Contracts

Major Felony Cases

Management Inspection

Management Labor Relations

Marriage Certificates

Material Handling

Media Relations

Mediations

Medical Documentation

Medium-Sized Law Firm

Memoranda

Memorandums of Law

Mental Health Law

Mentally Handicapped Clients

Misdemeanors

Modernization of Office
    Procedures

Money Orders

Monthly Logs

Mortgage Payment

Motions

Motor Vehicle Fraud

Municipal Buildings Security

Municipal Lien Certificates

Municipal Public Safety

Municipalities

Negotiation Strategies

Notarizing Legal Documents

Notice System

Official Records

On Foot

Outside Hospital Guard

Paralegal Services

Patients

Patrol

Peace

Perjury

Permitting Processes

Personal Effects

Physical Status

Plaintiffs

Plea Agreements

Policies and Procedures

Policing Functions

Polygraph Techniques

Population Counts

Post-Closing Functions

Powers of Arrest

Practice

Precedent Information

Pre-Disposition Conferences

Preparation of Cases

Pre-Trial Conference

Prioritize Assignments

Prisoner Visitation

Prisoners

Private Interests

Private Sector

Procedural Issues

Proceedings

Procurement Inspection

Production

Proper Operation

Properties

Property Cases

Property Matters

Proposed Findings

Prosecute

Protection

Provision of Security

Public Agency

Public Interests

Public Relations

Public Safety

Transactional Experience	Vandalism and Theft Deterrence
Transactions	Vendors
Transfer	Victims
Treatment Programs	Violating the Law
Trial	Volunteers
Trial Attorney	Weaponry Training
Trial Papers	Witnesses
Trial Preparation	Work Schedules
Trial Proceedings	Workload
Uniformed Commercial Code	Work-Study
Union Members	Writing Skills

COMMONLY USED ACTION VERBS:

Actuated	Initiated	Prosecuted
Advised	Interviewed	Protected
Argued	Negotiated	Represented
Conducted	Patrolled	Retained
Coordinated	Practiced	Served
Designed	Prepared	Supervised
Directed	Presented	Trained

ACTION VERBS AND BUZZ WORDS USED IN CONTEXT:

- *Prosecuted criminal cases* at *district court* in conjunction with *Urban Violence Strike Force.*

- *Prepared* and *presented* civil and *criminal motions* before *District* and *Superior Courts.*

- *Presented public-safety workshops* and lectures.

- *Supervised criminal investigations* and *trained assistant district attorneys.*

CHAPTER TWENTY-ONE

MARKETING AND SALES

BUZZ WORDS FOR POSITIONS in the fields of marketing and sales highlight experience with attracting customers, promoting businesses and increasing their public profiles, and closing deals. For these results-oriented positions, specific references to measurable accomplishments are most effective.

COMMON POSITIONS INCLUDE:

Account Executive	Marketing Assistant
Account Manager	Merchandising Manager
Account Representative	Product Developer
Ad Copywriter	Purchasing Agent
Advertising Assistant	Regional Account Manager
Advertising Coordinator	Regional Sales Manager
Advertising Manager	Retail Buyer
Callback Representative	Sales Administrator
Insurance Agent	Sales Assistant
Manufacturing Representative	Sales Executive
Market Research Analyst	Sales Manager
Marketing and Sales Director	Telemarketer

Telemarketing Director

Vice-President of Marketing

Vice-President of Sales

Wholesale Buyer

RESUME BUZZ WORDS:

4-Color Process

Account Acquisition

Account Balances

Account Locations

Account Performance

Accountable Documents

Accounting Noting Systems

Accounting Operations

Accounting Reports

Accounts

Accounts Receivables

Acquisition

Additional Business

Additional Sales

Adjusters

Adjustments

Administrative and Marketing
  Responsibilities

Administrative Policies

Administrative Procedures

Advertisement Placement

Advertisements

Advertising

Advertising Budget

Advertising Campaigns

Advertising Lineage

Advertising Positioning

Advertising Space

Advertising Strategy

Advertorials

After-Market Volume

After-Sales Support

Aggressive Work Flow
  Management

Analysis

Analysis of Current Accounts

Analysis of Old Accounts

Annual Ad Placements

Annual Division Sales

Annual Marketing Budget

Annual Purchases

Annual Sales

Annual Volume

Appointments

Area Trade

Assets

Assigned Sales Quotas

Average Annual Sales

Average Unit Sales

Awareness

Banking

Bank-Wide Advertising

Basement Store

Behavior-Based Research Projects

Benefits Administration Software
Biannual Sales Conferences
Billboard
Billing
Booking
Booking Agency
Booths
Branch Profits
Brand Initiative
Brochure Production
Brochures
Broker Accounts
Brokerage Concerns
Budget Controls
Budget Management
Budget Recommendation
Budgets
Business Accounts
Business Contacts
Business Expansion
Business Plan
Business Protocols
Business Relationships
Business Reviews
Business-to-Business Services
Buyers
Buying Trips
Camera Ready Ads
Cash Transactions
Catalogues
Centralized Reporting System

Claim Settlements
Claims Handling
Claims Service
Classified Advertising
Client Base
Client Confidence
Client Needs
Client Relations
Client Service
Clients
Closing
Closing Capabilities
Cluster Analysis
Cold Call Sales Generation
    Centers
Cold Calling
Collateral Materials
Collection
Color Brochures
Commerce
Commercial Products
Commercial Properties
Commission Checks
Commissions
Communication Audits
Communication Network
Company Development
Company Distribution Center
Company Management Structure
Company Procedures
Company Purchase Agreements

Company/Customer Personnel
Competitive Pricing
Competitive Ranking
Comprehensive Expertise
Computer Estimating Software
   Package
Concept Testing
Confidential Reports
Constituency Relations
Consulting Firms
Consumer Behavior Models
Consumer Goods
Consumer Oriented
Consumer Products
Contract Negotiations
Contract Options
Contracted Vendors
Contracts
Contractual Reversions
Controller
Cooperative Sales Strategy
Core Products
Corporate Accounts
Corporate Chain
Corporate Clients
Corporate Contacts
Corporate Field Contact
Corporate Financial Management
Corporate Objectives
Corporate Plans
Corporate Position

Correspondence
Cost Parameters
Cost-of-Lead
Counters
Creative Concept
Creative Ideas
Creative Services
Credit Checks
Current Pricing
Customer Base
Customer Buying Policies
Customer Follow-Up
Customer Inquiries
Customer Needs
Customer Package Specifications
Customer Relations
Customer Reservation
   Specification
Customer Satisfaction
Customer Satisfaction
   Measurement
Customer Service
Customer Service Procedures
Customer Service Techniques
Customer Specification
Customer Studies
Cycles
Daily Calendar History
Daily Deposits
Daily Interface With Clients
Daily Operations

Daily Reports

Daily Tax Title Receipts

Dealer Channels

Dealer Commission

Dealer Locations

Dealer Promotions

Decision Making Process

Deep Discount Stores

Department Procedures

Department Standards

Departmental Contracts

Design Concepts

Detailed Sales Forecasts

Determination of Costs

Development Projects

Direct Calls

Direct Claims Handling

Direct Liaison

Direct Mail Brochures

Direct Mail Promotions

Direct Mail Schedule

Direct Mail Strategy

Direct Marketing

Direct Sales

Display Techniques

Displays

Distribution

Distribution Disagreements

Diverse Specifications

Divisional Business Plan

Documentation

Dollar Volume

Domestic Calling Needs

Domestic Fares

Education Accounts

Elicit Interest

Employee Studies

Employee Training and
    Effectiveness Program

End-User Software

Engineering Solutions

Engineering Staff

Equipment Installation

Events Planning

Executive Relocations

Exhibit

Exhibit Posters

Exhibitions

Existing Accounts

Expense Account

Fabrication

Facilitate Sales

Factory Authorized Dealers

Field Coordination

Field Sales

Field Surveys

Final Itineraries

Finance

Financers

Financial Account

Financial Institutions

Financial Packages

Financial Statements

Financial Support Services

First Time Buyers

Flyers

Focus Group

Follow-Through

Follow-Up

Forecast

Foreclosure Sales

Foreign Customs

Freelance Models

Fundraising Capabilities

Future Action

Future Sales

General Accounting Functions

General Management

General Supplies Purchasing

Goals

Government Allotments

Government Contractor

Gross Sales

High Exposure Claims

High Motivational Level

High-End Sales

Historical Data Planbook

Immediate Goals

Incentive Programs

Incoming Calls

Incoming Invoices

Increase Sales

In-Depth Questionnaires

In-Depth Sales Training

Individual Sales Leads

Industry Knowledge

Industry Research

Industry Trends

Information Requests

In-House Promotions

Initial Business Plan

Innovative Techniques

In-Print Advertising Campaigns

In-Print Marketing Campaigns

Installation of Systems

Installed Accounts

Instrument Development

Intake Forms

Interior Displays

Internal Strategic Planning

International Calling Needs

International Distributors

International Fares

Interviewing Techniques

Inventory

Inventory Control System

Inventory Products

Investment Properties

Involved Parties

Key Account Relations

Key Account Sales

Key Accounts

Large Scale Development

Large Scale Investments

Lead Analysis

Leads

Leasing

Legal Documents

Legal Requirements

Leisure Accounts

Letters of Intent

License Regulatory Issues

Licensees

Lines of Merchandise

Local Franchises

Local Promotions

Long Range Business Planning

Long Term Contracts

Long Term Goals

Loss Performance

Loss Prevention Programs

Loss Report Reviews

Low Turnover Rate

Major Accounts

Major Manufacturers

Major Wholesalers

Management Reports

Management Systems

Manufacturing Requests

Market Analysis

Market Conditions

Market Enthusiasm

Market Opportunities

Market Research

Market Segment

Market Share

Market Trends

Marketing

Marketing Campaigns

Marketing Effort

Marketing Expenses

Marketing Information

Marketing Materials

Marketing Plans

Marketing Promotions

Marketing Research and Analysis

Marketing Research Needs

Marketing Segmentation

Marketing Strategies

Marketing Support Operations

Marketing Technology

Mass Marketing

Mass Merchandising

Maximize Sales

Media Contracts

Media Coverage

Media Department

Media Events

Media Files

Merchandising

Merchandising Concepts

Merchandising Functions

Merchandising Materials

Merchandising Products

Merchants

Mid-Size Companies

Monthly Claims Quota

Monthly Communications
    Packages

Monthly Forecast

Monthly Planbook

Monthly Sales Plan

Multiethnic Population

Multimillion-Dollar Negotiations

Multivariate Techniques

Name/Logo Testing

National Account

National Probability Survey

National Sales Strategy

Nationwide Network

Negotiate

Net Operating Profit

Net Profit Margins

New Business Development

New Business Technology

New Clients

New Product

New Product Launch

New Product Research

Newsletters

Newspaper Ad System

Newspaper Inserts

Nonprofit Accounts

Ongoing Customer Relationships

On-Site Survey Groups

Open-Order Status Reports

Operating Plans

Operational Budgets

Operational Deadlines

Operational Procedures

Order Accuracy

Order Placement

Order Processing

Orders

Outlet Sales

Outside Sales

Outstanding Performance

Overall Market Strategy

Overall Sales Efforts

Parallel Exporting

Parallel Processing

Percentages

Performance

Performance Evaluations

Performance Incentives

Periodic Claims Reviews

Personal Account Information

Personal Relations

Pertinent Materials

Petitions of Foreclosure

Placement

Point of Sales Forecasting

Policy

Portfolio Objectives

Portfolios

Positioning

Positive Company Image

Post Installation Analysis

Posters

Potential Business Applications

Potential Clients

Pre-Booked Sales

Pre-Qualification

Press Clippings

Press Kits

Press Releases

Price

Price Selections

Pricing Data

Primary Emphasis

Print Licenses

Print Marketing

Print Production

Private Investors

Procedures

Procurement Negotiation

Product Awareness

Product Development Operations

Product Enhancements

Product Knowledge

Product Line Presentation

Product Merchandising

Product Packages

Product Presentations

Product Recognition

Product Requirements

Product Sales

Product Training

Product Usage

Production

Production Schedules

Professional Growth

Professional Sales

Profit Estimates

Profitable Line

Profitable Relationships

Program Commitment

Program Performance

Project Specification

Promotional Agencies

Promotional Concept

Promotional Copy

Promotional Events

Promotional Material

Promotional Strategies

Promotional Work

Promotions

Proof

Proposal Preparation

Proposals

Prospect Identification

Prospecting

Prospective Clients

Provision of Sales Services

Public Relations

Publicity Opportunities

Purchaser/User Studies

Qualified Clients

Qualified Prospects

Quality Performance

Quality Product

Quantitative Research Projects

Quarterly Budget Reports

Quarterly Forecasts

Quota Assignment

Quota Expectations

Quoting System

Radio Marketing

Rapid-Growth Organization

Rate Structure

Ratebook

Reactivation of Dormant
  Accounts

Real Estate Companies

Real Estate Development
  Division

Real Estate Sales

Real-Time Market Data

Recurring Revenue Agreements

Referral

Registration Data

Releases

Remote Market Information

Remote Markets

Remote Territory

Rental Contracts

Rentals

Research Laboratories

Resellers

Residential Consumers

Retail Buying

Retail Outlets

Retail Sales

Retailing

Revenue Streams

Round-Table Discussions

Salary Reviews

Sales Aids

Sales Appointments

Sales Campaigns

Sales Candidate

Sales Collateral

Sales Conventions

Sales Efforts

Sales Goals

Sales Objective

Sales Per Year

Sales Plan

Sales Presentations

Sales Priorities

Sales Production

Sales Productivity

Sales Programs

Sales Projections

Sales Promotions

Sales Results

Sales Scripts

Sales Services

Sales Support

Sales Techniques

Sales Volume

Sales/Marketing Copy

Sample Development
Seasonal Merchandise
Seasonal Planbook
Seasonal Planning
Selling Reports
Seminars
Service Accounts
Short Range Business Planning
Software Vendor
Source Selections
Space Ads
Special Advertising
Special Assignment
Special Events
Special Ordering
Special Requests
Special Seasonal Sales
Specialty Book Club Licenses
Sponsor Relations
Stock
Stock Areas
Stock Control
Stock Levels
Store Chains
Strategic Planning
Subcontractors
Subsidiary Rights Contracts
Subsidiary Rights Licenses
Subsidiary Rights Monies
Supplement Program
Support Networks

Support Services
Tally Sheets
Tapes
Target Accounts
Target Grids
Target Market
Technical and Cost Proposals
Technical Presentations
Technical Sales
Technical Sales Support
Tele-Interviewing
Telemarketing
Telemarketing Scripts
Telephone Techniques
Terms
Territory
Third-Party Distribution
    Channels
Timely Merchandising Delivery
Top Account Executives
Top Sales Performer
Total Client Satisfaction
Total Quality Implementation
Total Volume
Tour Schedules
Track Record
Trade Shows
Training Record
Transaction Data
Travel Orders
Union Labor

Unit Pricing

Unmarked Territory

Upwardly Mobile Buyers

User Friendly

Valuable Application

Value of Claim

Vendor Programs

Vendors

Verbal Sales Skills

Vertical Market Framework

Viable Network

Visual Appeal

Volume Increase

Warehouse

Warehouse Accountability

Warehouse Administration

Weekly Planbook

Well-Traveled

Well-Established

Wide Range

Window Displays

Wire Trades

Working Knowledge

Working Relationships

Work-Sheet Program

Workshops

Workstations

Written Communication Skills

Yearly Sales Activity

Year-To-Date Sales

Commonly Used Action Verbs:

Coordinated

Created

Designed

Devised

Directed

Edited

Executed

Generated

Implemented

Initiated

Interacted

Maintained

Managed

Operated

Organized

Planned

Prepared

Sold

Supervised

Updated

Action Verbs and Buzz Words Used in Context:

- *Managed* the *sale* of *products* into *dealer locations*.

- *Initiated* *cooperative sales strategy* with *reseller business owners*, *designed* *marketing promotions*, and *directed* *reseller's sales efforts* into business and education *accounts*.

- *Supervised* staff of *copywriters* and *managed* activities of *designers*, *photographers*, and *printers*.

- *Generated* *confidential reports* and monthly *communication packages*; *interacted* with *Production Department* and *store managers*.

- *Contacted* members to rent *booths*, *sent promotional materials* to *buyers*, and *contracted* for *media advertising*.

- *Addressed* all *marketing research needs*, e.g., *marketing segmentation*, *concept testing*, and *product usage and awareness*.

- *Managed behavior-based research projects* including *proposal writing*; *methodology*, *instrument*, *and sample development*; *field coordination*; *data coding*; *analysis* and interpretation; report writing.

CHAPTER TWENTY-TWO

PRINTING AND PUBLISHING

PRINTING AND PUBLISHING buzz words display experience and familiarity with content management, book and magazine production, printing environments, and applicable technologies and systems.

COMMON POSITIONS INCLUDE:

Carrier Route Driver

Classified Sales Representative

Copy Editor

Customer Service
Representative

Development Editor

Director of Photography

Driver

Inserter

Journals Acquisitions Editor

Journals Assistant

Marketing Operations
Coordinator

Marketing Research Manager

Multimedia Analyst

Network Television
Distribution Analyst

Prepress Operator

Production Manager

Project Editor

Research Analyst

Sales Representative

RESUME BUZZ WORDS:

Academia

Academic Books

Acquiring Authors

Acquiring Books

Adult Secondary and Primary
   Material

Advance

Advertising Specialties

Agents

Animation

Announcements

Annual Reports

Aptitude Tests

Art Design

Artwork Services

Authoring Process

Authors

Backlist

Billing and Payment

Billing Orders

Binders

Bindery Equipment

Binding

Block Printing

Boiler Plate

Book Manufacturing

Book Production

Brochures

Bundling

Business Forms

Business Stationery

Cable Television

Calligraphy

Camera-Ready Graphics

Catalog Copy

Catalogs

Character

Children's Books

Circulation

Color Correction

Color Forms

Commercial Printing

Communications Firm

Communications Systems

Consumer Magazine Publishing

Content Edit

Contract

Converting Process

Copy Edit

Corporate Printing

Corporate Publishing System

Counting

Course Needs

Cover Copy

Custom Publishing

Customer Accounts

Customer Needs

Daily Newspapers

Data Entry
Data Manipulation Services
Database Development
Deal Sheet
Design
Detail-Oriented
Developing Books
Dictionaries
Digital Color
Digital Fonts
Digital Media Input
Direct Mailing
Directories
Distribution
Distribution Technology
Document Library Services
Document Management
Documentation Services
EDI (Electronic Data
    Interchange)
Editing
Editorial Calendar
Editorial Literary Services
Editorial Materials
Editorial Process
Editorial Vision
Educational Material
Electronic Archiving
Electronic Printer
Electronic Production
Electronic Publishing

Electronic Storage and Retrieval
    Systems
Electrotype
Encyclopedias
Engraved Plate
Engraved Rollers
Fiction
Fiction Book Publisher
Film
Financial Printing
Formats
Formatting
Fulfillment Services
Full-Color Process
Galleys
Guides
Handbills
Hardcover
High-Production Environment
High-Speed Digital Printers
High-Volume Photocopying
Illustrations
Imaging
Impression
Imprints
Independent Publishers
Information Management
Information Services
Informational Publications
Ink
Ink Jetting

Inked Type

Instructional Materials

Integrated Circulation Services

Internet Content Publishing

Inventory Management

ISO9002 Certification

Ivory Black

Laminating

Lampblack

Large Format

Laser Imaging

Layout

Legal Printing

Lettering

Libraries

Library Information Science

List Acquisition

List Management

Literary Fiction

Literary Manuscripts

Lithographic Stone

Local Distribution

Logos

Magazines

Mailing

Manuals

Market Research

Market Share Analysis

Market Studies

Marketing Collateral

Marketing Services Company

Markings

Mass Market Paperback

Matter

Media

Media Buying

Media Planning

Medical Books and Journals

Mission Critical Data

Movie

Multimedia Products

Multiple Machine Environments

Musical Piece

Negatives

Network-Affiliated TV Stations

New Title Development

News-Gathering

Newsletters

Newswire Service

Nonfiction

Nonfiction Book Publishers

Offset

Online Library

Online Sports Information

Outside Vendors

Package

Packaging and Finishing

Pagination

Pamphlets

Parcel Fulfillment

Perfect Bind

Periodicals

Photo Retouching

Photographic Image

Photography

Photosensitive Surface

Pickup and Delivery

Plates

Poems

Poetry

Post Press

PostScript Files

Presentations

Press

Presswork

Primary Source Material

Printed Material

Printing

Printing Frame

Printing House

Printing Ink

Printing Paper

Printing Press

Printing Wheel

Print-on-Demand

Print-Production

Production Costs

Production Environment

Production Process

Professional Production Services

Professional Testing Products and
Services

Project Costs

Project Management Experience

Promotional Activities

Promotional and Premium
Copies

Promotional Copy

Prose

Public Attention

Public Contact

Public Distribution

Publication Layout

Publicity

Published Work

Publisher

Quick Conversion

Quote Generation

Radio Data Terminals

Real-Time Financial Market Data

Replication Services

Reprints

Reproduction Process

Research

Retouching

Roll Systems

Royalties

Scanning

Schedules and Quality
Guidelines

Scholarly Books

Science Textbooks

Seal

Sensitized Paper

Short Run Books

Single-Source Marketing Organization

Small Press Publishers

Software Packaging

Sorting

Specialty Publishers

Specs

Stacking

Stamp

Statistical Information

Stereotype

Subscriptions

Subsidiary Ledgers

Supplements

Targeting Strategies

Technical and Reference Books

Technical Manuals

Text Books

Text Capture Services

The Press

Third Party Publishers

Titles

Trade Publications

Trucking

Turnaround Time

TV Broadcasting Services

Typesetting

Typing Ability

Typography

University Presses

Verses

Warehousing Books

Web Publishers

Weeklies

Wire-O Books

Wood Block

Workflow

Yearbooks

COMMONLY USED ACTION VERBS:

Acquired

Advertised

Announced

Conceived

Declared

Disclosed

Divulged

Edited

Executed

Issued

Maintained

Negotiated

Prepared

Printed

Proclaimed

Produced

Promulgated

Proofed

Read

Revealed

Trafficked

Wrote

ACTION VERBS AND BUZZ WORDS USED IN CONTEXT:

- *Conceived* and *executed book ideas*, following up with *author representatives* and closing deals.

- *Maintained* contact with *authors* and *cultivated* contact with *literary agents*.

- *Participated* in *editorial* and *sales meetings* and *worked* closely with sales, marketing, art and design, and production departments as required.

- *Wrote* and *edited jacket copy* and *sales and marketing materials*.

- *Trafficked manuscripts* throughout the entire *editorial process* from *initial submission* to *bound book*.

- *Managed* a team of *copy editors*, ensuring adherence to *grammar*, *quality standards*, and *styles*.

- *Acquired* twenty new *nonfiction titles* each year.

- *Established* and *maintained* relationships with *writers* and *agents*.

- *Negotiated contract* and *publishing terms*.

- *Researched* and *wrote* about news and trends affecting the *publishing industry*.

- *Directed supplement program* of over seventy *books* from budget management to project completion with specific emphasis on *electronic manuscript preparation*.

CHAPTER TWENTY-THREE

REAL ESTATE

BUZZ WORDS FOR POSITIONS in this field highlight experience acting as a medium for transactions between homebuyers and sellers. They should show knowledge in evaluating the construction of a home in order to estimate its market value; contacting individuals by phone, mail, or in person to interview and assist them in completing various forms; and verifying the information obtained and performing various processing tasks. This often includes knowledge of leasing laws, contracts, and mortgages.

COMMON POSITIONS INCLUDE:

Administrative Coordinator

Agent

Appraiser

Asset Manager

Assistant Property Director

Broker

Contractor

Director of Property
  Management

Finance Advisor

Financial Analyst

Investment Sales Manager

Leasing Consultant

Leasing Manager

Licensed Conveyancer

Loan Officer

Mortgage Loan Lender

Property Financial Analyst

Real Estate Inspector

Real Estate Paralegal

Real Estate Salesperson

Realtor

Sales Director

RESUME BUZZ WORDS:

Abandonment

Acquisitions

Active Adult Communities

Adjustable Rate

Adjustment

Adult Retirement Communities

Advisory Services

Agency

Agreement

Apartment Buildings

Apartment Communities

Apartment Sales

Apartments

Applications

Applications Processing

Appraisals

Approvals

Asking Price

Asset Management Services

Asset Value

Assets

Assignment

Assisted Living Centers

Audits

Balance

Bankruptcy

Base Salary

Beneficiary

Bill of Sale

Binder

Blanket Mortgage

Bonds

Breach

Brokerage

Budget Forecasts

Buffer Zone

Building Code

Buying

By Owner

Capital Gain

Certificate of Title

Clause

Clients

Closing

Code of Ethics

Collateral

Colonial

Commercial

Commercial Office Space

Commission

Common Law

Company Policy

Institutional Buildings

Institutional Investors

Insurance

Insurance Claims

Integrated

Interest

Interest Rate

Investment Trust

Investments

Joint Tenancy

Land

Lease

Lease-Up

Leasing

Leasing Goals

Leasing Operation

Lessee

Lessor

Leverage

License

Liens

Listing

Loans

Locations

Loft

Long-Term

Long-Term Care Services

Luxury Housing

Maintenance

Major Metropolitan Area

Management Firm

Market Research

Market Value

Marketing

Markets

Master Planning

Metropolitan

Mid-Priced Single-Family Homes

Mobile Homes

Mortgage

Mortgage Loans

Motels

Move-Ins

Multifamily Properties

Multifamily Property
   Management

Multitenanted Property

Notes

Nursing Homes

Office

Office Buildings

Open House

Owner Financing

Partial Payment

Performance Reviews

Personal Property

Plazas

Point

Power of Attorney

Pre-Approval

Prepayment

Pre-Qualification

Taxes	Transactions
Tenancy	Turnover
Tenancy-at-Will	Unit
Third-Party Property Owners	Vacancies
Title	Vendor Relations
Title Insurance	Work Orders
Trailer Parks	

COMMONLY USED ACTION VERBS

Advised	Directed	Reviewed
Appraised	Explained	Showed
Assessed	Handled	Sold
Bought	Negotiated	Specialized
Calculated	Obtained	Toured
Conducted	Processed	Updated
Contracted	Refinanced	Worked

ACTION VERBS AND BUZZ WORDS USED IN CONTEXT:

- **Showed** *apartments* and *condominiums* to potential *clients* at *open houses*.

- **Worked** directly with *real estate brokers* on *property acquisitions*.

- **Drew up** *leases* and *tenancy at will agreements* for *closings*.

- **Kept** lists of *current vacancies*, **responded** to work orders and **directed** *maintenance* crews to problem areas, and **handled** all *residential relations*.

- **Conducted** audits of *real estate brokers and agents*; **reviewed** tax records and *turnover rates*.

- *Specialized* in *securities portfolio management*, advising *clients* interested in investing in *commercial real estate*.

- *Contracted construction projects* of *subdivisions* and *trailer parks* to suit marketed demographic needs.

- *Handled security deposits and refunds*, *processed purchase agreements*, *updated listings* in local newspapers, and *oversaw* bookkeeping for *rent collection*.

- *Reviewed loan applications*, *ran credit checks*, *appraised property values* for *market release*, and *advised* clients on *tenancy agreements*.

- *Directed* sales team on *pitching strategies*, *obtaining exclusive listings*, and *negotiating asking prices*.

- *Negotiated sales prices* of *studios* with *estate owners* during *acquisitions periods*.

- *Advised lessees* on *locations*, rates, *tenancy agreements*, and all other aspects of rental processes.

- *Conducted market research* to determine average *real estate sales* and *rental rates* on a weekly basis.

- *Sold office buildings* upon *renovations* that brought them up to *building code* at a *fair market value*.

CHAPTER TWENTY-FOUR

RETAIL

RETAIL INDUSTRY BUZZ WORDS
demonstrate experience in the sale of clothing, goods, or appliances, either directly to consumers or to the retail stores, or the buying of such products for sale in stores. They also demonstrate knowledge of customer service, handling transactions, complaints, and returns, and the management of a retail environment.

COMMON POSITIONS INCLUDE:

Assistant Store Manager	Internal Auditor
Associate Buyer	Inventory Control Analyst
Assortment Management Planner	Market Coordinator
	Merchandise Manager
Auto Technician	Merchandiser
Buyer	Planner
Cashier	Regional Manager
Delivery Driver	Relationships Manager
Department Lead	Sales Associate
District Manager	Stock Associate
District Training Store Manager	Store Manager
Divisional Operations Director	Warehouse Worker

RESUME BUZZ WORDS:

Accessories

Accounts Receivable

Advertising

Advertising Programs

American Designers

Annual Circulation

Antiques

Apparel

Appliances

Art

Assortments

Audio Equipment

Automobiles

Automotive

Automotive Aftermarket
  Products

Automotive Manufacturers

Back Order

Baking Facilities

Barcode

Beauty Care Products

Bedroom Sets

Book Titles

Bookstores

Boutique

Branch

Brand Names

Building Materials

Buyback

Call Recording Devices

Camera Shop

Car Audio Systems

Cash On Delivery

Cash Register

Cash Register Tape

Cash Transaction

Casual Apparel

Catalog Retailer

Cataloger

Categories

Cellular Phones

Children

Children's Active Wear

Children's Products

Christmas Products

City-Style Apparel

Classic Apparel

Clearance Sale

Clothing

Coatings

Collegiate Department Store

Company-Owned

Computers

Consumer

Consumer Advocate

Cookware

Co-Operative

Copy Center

Cost

Credit Card Transactions

Customers

Daily Sales Audit

Decorative Products

Delicatessen

Demo

Department Store

Department Store Merchandise

Design

Design Professionals

Desks

Dining Room Sets

Direct Mail Software

Direct Marketing

Direct Selling

Discount Bookstore Chain

Discount Drugs

Discount Office Products

Discount Outlet

Discounted Prices

Distressed Goods

Doors and Windows

Dresses

Drug Store Products

Drugstores

Dry Cleaning

Electrical Supplies

Electronic Funds Transfer

Electronic Products

Electronics

End Caps

Exchange Policy

Exchanges

Fabric Retailer

Factory-Direct

Fad

Family Apparel

Fashion

Fashion Jewelry

Features

Floor Model

Focused Selection

Food Retailers

Food Service Distribution
 Businesses

Food Services

Footwear

Fragrances

Franchisees

Full-Line

Full-Line Department Store

Full-Price Stores

Furniture

Furniture Manufacturers

Gardening Products

Gas Stations

General Merchandise

Gift Certificate

Gift Products

Gift Receipt

Gifts

Global Retailer

Grocery Chains

Gross Margin

Hang Tag

Hardware

Headsets

Health and Fitness

High-Volume

Home and Safety

Home Audio Systems

Home Furnishings

Home Improvement Centers

Home Office Systems

Home Theater Speakers

Hosiery

Household Products

Housewares

Ice Cream

Ice Cream Manufacturer

Independent Dealers

Independent Operators

Independent Sales

    Representatives

Independently Owned

Industrial Maintenance Market

Initial Markup

International Designers

Inventory

Item Price Marking

Kiosk

Kitchen Furniture

Knitted Fabrics

Label

Layaway

Leading Retailer

Leased

Leisurewear

Licensed Franchises

Limited Warranty

Line Switches

Lingerie

Living Room Sets

Locations

Loss Prevention

Lumber

Mail-Order Retailing

Mail-Order Apparel

Mall

Mall-Based Retail Outlets

Management Support Designed

Mannequin

Manufactures

Markdown

Marketing

Marketing Research

Markets

Markup

Mass Merchandisers

Material

Meat Processing

Member-Owned

Men

Merchandise

Merchandising

Milk-Processing Plant

Moderately Priced Merchandise

Music

Music Departments

National Direct Sales Company

Nationally Recognized Brands

Network

No Frills

Office Products

Off-Price Outlet Stores

Off-Price Retail

Online Sales

Original Equipment
    Manufacturers (OEM)

Outdoor and Garden
    Merchandise

Paint

Percentage

Personal Care Products

Photo Development Services

Photographic Equipment

Plumbing Supplies

Price Marketing

Price War

Prints

Private Labels

Product Line

Products

Promotion

Promotional Advertising

Promotional Discount

Quantity Discount

Ready-To-Assemble

Receipt

Refund

Related Support Facilities

Reserve Stock

Retail Chain

Retail Convenience Stores

Retail Drug Stores

Retail Fabric Stores

Retail Furniture Stores

Retail Locations

Retail Price

Retail Units

Retail Warehouse Stores

Retailer

Returns

Sales Forecasting

Sales Promotion

Seasonal Discount

Selected Home Furnishings

Serving Equipment

Shoe Departments

Site Location

Soft-Goods Products

Software

Specialty Catalog Retailer

Specialty Catalogs

Specialty Clothing

Specialty Fashion Store

Specialty Men's Wear

Specialty Paint and Wall
Covering Stores

Specialty Retailer

Specialty Women's Clothing
Retailer

Sportswear

Stereo

Store Chain

Store Credit

Store Items

Suggestive Selling

Super Drug Stores

Supermarket Chain

Superstores

Swimwear

Target Market

Telephone Productivity Items

Telephones

Televisions

Toys

Trade

Traffic Paint Market

Travel and Luggage

Trend

Tuxedo

Unit-Of-Sale Method

Universal Product Code (UPC)

Used

Value-Priced

Various Industries

Video Rental

Videos

Warehouse Foods

Warehouses

Warranty

Wholesale

Wholly Owned Subsidiaries

Wide Assortments

Wide Variety

Women's Apparel

Women's Intimate-Apparel

Work Clothing

Woven Fabrics

COMMONLY USED ACTION VERBS:

Bought	Inventoried	Oversaw
Catalogued	Managed	Priced
Excelled	Marketed	Scheduled
Explained	Operated	Served
Filled	Ordered	Shipped
Helped	Organized	Sold

ACTION VERBS AND BUZZ WORDS USED IN CONTEXT:

- *Explained* brands of televisions, videos, cellular phones, computers, and other *electronics* to *customers*.

- *Filled* orders, *shipped* products, and *answered* calls for *women's intimate apparel catalog retailer*.

- *Operated* cash register, ringing both *cash and credit card transactions*, with responsibility for knowledge of *discounted prices*, *clearance items*, *ad items*, and changes in *universal product codes (UPCs)*.

- *Managed* specialty fashion store carrying *private label product lines* of *nationally recognized brands*.

- *Sold* wide assortment of *primary apparel* in *mall-based retail outlet* at *value prices*.

- *Bought* women's, men's, and children's apparel for *independently owned retail store*.

- *Excelled* in *suggestive selling* of *sales promotions*, as well as *customer service* duties, such as *layaways*, *returns*, and *exchanges*.

- *Organized* shipments of *accessories*, *stocked* shelves by categories in different departments, and *took inventory* of all items annually.

- *Oversaw* all aspects of managing one location in major *bookstore chain*, including verifying *barcodes*, organizing *category sections* by book title, *scheduling* employees, and handling all accounting.

CHAPTER TWENTY-FIVE

SCIENCE

FOR SCIENTIFIC POSITIONS, each particular field will have many specialized technical terms aside from those listed here. Science industry buzz words, in general, display experience with research and development. This includes research to develop new medicines; increase crop yield; improve the environment; study farm crops, animals, and living organisms; and explore practical use and knowledge of chemicals, as well as the atmosphere's physical characteristics, motions, and processes.

COMMON POSITIONS INCLUDE:

Agricultural Scientist	Geophysicist
Astronomer	Laboratory Assistant
Chemist	Laboratory Technician
Chemistry Research Assistant	Marine Biologist
Conservation Scientist	Meteorologist
Farm Manager	Physicist
Forest Scientist	Research Associate
Forester/Park Ranger	Science Writer
Geologist	Zoologist

RESUME BUZZ WORDS:

Aberrations

Absolute Molecular Weight

Acreage Evaluation

Agrarian-Based Industries

Agriculture

Air Pollution

Algal Organisms

Amphibious Surveying Operation

Analysis

Animal Care

Animal Health Practices

Animal Husbandry

Animals

Annual Operating Budget

Aquaculture Projects

Arborists

Artificial Insemination
    Considerations

Assisted Animals

Bacteria

Bale

Beef

Bid Documents

Binary Stars

Biochemical Procedures

Biochemistry

Biological Research

Biological Sources

Blood Banking Procedures

Blood Components

Blood Products

Branching Data

Breeding

Briefing Papers

Briefings

Brillouin Scattering

Briquetting

Cadmium Telluride Gamma Ray
    Detector

Calculations

Carcinogenic Analysis

Cellular Structure

Ceramics

Chemical Synthetic Procedures

Chemicals

Chemistry

Classroom-Style Lectures

Cleanup Procedures

Coastline

Common Illnesses

Compositions

Comprehensive Management
    Plan

Computer Record Maintenance

Computerized Assays

Continuous Viscometer Detector

Contractual Services

Courses

Fisheries

Flood Protection

Foaling

Forecasting Weather

Forecasts

Forestry

Forests

Fungal Cell Metabolism

Funnel Extractions

Gel Permeation Chromatography

Genetic Factors

Genetic Research

Genetics

Geological Aspects

Geological Background

Geophysical Crew

Geophysical Exploration
    Programs

Glacial Deposits

Grant Tracking Support

Grooming

Ground Water

Growth Parameters

Hay

Heat Treatment

Heavy Mineral Separation

Helium Neon Laser

Herbicides

Hormonal Assays

Horticultural Planting

Horticulture

Hospital Laboratories

Hubble Telescope

Humidity

Hurricanes

Industrial Wastes

Instrument Automation

Instrumentation

Inventory

Invertebrate

Irrigation

Isolation Schemes

Lab

Lab Samples

Labeling

Labor

Laboratories

Laboratory Inventory

Laboratory Operations

Laboratory Setting

Lamb

Lambing Season

Large-Scale Fermentation

Light Mineral Separation

Light Weight Aggregates

Lime Manufacturer

Livestock

Local Dairies

Lumber Projects

Magnitude

Mainframe System

Maintenance Schedules

Plant Alkaloids

Plants

Plasmid Constructions

Plasmid DNA Purification

Positron Annihilation
    Spectroscopy

Precipitation Level

Preparing Media

Private Sectors

Privately Funded Organizations

Process Experimentation

Produce

Produce Farm

Production Basis

Production Handling

Proper Calibration

Protein Assays

Protein Purification

Proteins

Pruning

Q Switched Ruby Laser

Quality Control Systems

Radar

Radiosonic Equipment

Raw Material

Recombinant DNA Technology

Research and Development

Research Papers

Research Problems

Research Reports

Research Techniques

Ribosome Structure

RNA Component

Sanitation Procedures

Satellites

Science Texts

Scientific Crew

Scientific Seminars

Sea Transportation

Seasonal Climate Conditions

Seeds

Semiconductor Neutron Detector

Semiconductors

SI Mapping

Slides

Soil Samples

Soil Testing

Special Forecasts

Specialized Instrumentation

Specialized Test Equipment

Stars' Magnitudes

Steroids

Stimulated Sound Scattering

Studs

Study Subjects

Subsurface

Supernovae

Surface Stations

Surrogate Solutions

Surveying

Technical Applications

Technical Data

Technical Writing	U.S. Wildlife Department
Telescope	Upper-Air Data
Temperature	Upper-Air Stations
Territorial Logging	USDA Regulations
Test Results	Vaccination Schedules
Tests	Vegetation
Textbook	Veterinary Medicine
T-Flasks	Viral Immunology Testing
Thoroughbreds	Vitamins
Tilapia	Waste Disposal
Timber	Waste Water
Tissue Culture Glassware	Water Supply
Tissue Experiment	Weather Balloon
Total Maintenance Program	Weather Conditions
Toxicity Tests	Weed Control
Trace Organic Analysis	Well Logging
Traces	Wet Chemistry
Transfusion	Wildlife
Tree Acquisition	Wildlife Activities
Trees	Winds
Turf Management	Zoo

COMMONLY USED ACTION VERBS:

Built	Evaluated	Processed
Completed	Examined	Promoted
Conducted	Filtered	Recorded
Designed	Handled	Researched
Developed	Monitored	Sterilized
Diagnosed	Originated	Supported
Ensured	Performed	Tested

ACTION VERBS AND BUZZ WORDS USED IN CONTEXT:

- *Ensured* smooth running of the *lab* and orderly maintenance of *telescopes*; *ordered equipment* and *supplies*.

- *Conducted* more than 500 *manual and computerized assays* of *steroids, carcinogenic analysis, vitamins, fibrinogens*, and other *chemicals* in *hospital laboratory*.

- *Developed laboratory microcomputer systems* for *instrument automation* and custom and specialized *instrumentation/test equipment*.

- *Designed* and *built* a *continuous viscometer detector* for *gel permeation chromatography* to provide *absolute molecular weight* and *branching data*.

- *Performed set funnel extractions*, creating *surrogate solutions* and maintaining *laboratory inventory* of glassware and *chemicals, waste disposal*, and *cleanup*.

- *Managed* the operation of a *livestock and production farm*, its marketing and accounting tasks, selling *beef, lamb*, and *produce* to supermarkets, restaurants, and roadside vegetable stands.

- *Researched* sources for *tree and plant acquisition*.

- *Made* written, editorial, and *research contributions* to ten *briefing papers* and a *comprehensive management plan* for Puget Sound.

- *Worked* directly with doctors of *veterinary medicine* and *racehorse trainers* in the breeding and grooming of top-quality *thoroughbreds*.

CHAPTER TWENTY-SIX

SERVICE

THESE SERVICE INDUSTRY BUZZ words highlight experience with providing high-quality customer service. This includes positions in food preparation, clerical work, retail, and the like. For more food-related buzz words, see Chapter Fourteen; for buzz words related to hotels, see also Chapter Seventeen.

COMMON POSITIONS INCLUDE:

Associate	Flight Attendant
Attendant	Food Inspector
Cashier	Hairstylist
Caterer	Health Club Manager
Chef	Hotel Clerk
Cosmetologist	Hotel Concierge
Customer Service Manager	Hotel Manager
Customer Service	Restaurant Manager
Representative	Sanitation Inspector
Fast Food Worker	Wait Person

RESUME BUZZ WORDS:

Academic Training

Account Adjustment

Accounting

Accounting Principles

Address Changes

Adjustments

Administrative Policies

Advice

Analysis of Services

Assisting Customers

Attractive Presentations

Automated Solutions

Banquets

Base Salary

Bill Maintenance and
Reconciliation

Billing

Billing Process

Bookings

Booth Set-Up

Budget

Budget Worksheets

Business Conventions

Business Management

Business Practices

Business Protocol

Business System Support

Business System Training

Cash Control

Cash Deposits

Cash Intake

Cash Received

Cash Reconciliations

Cash Transactions

Cashiering

Centralized Management
Systems

Check-In

Checkout

Client Base

Client Needs

Clientele

Clients

Cold Calling

Commercial Account Installation

Commitment to Excellence

Community Development

Complete and Thorough Service

Confidential Client Files

Conflict Resolution

Consulting with Guests

Consumer Services

Contract Negotiation

Corporate Accounts

Corporate Communication

Corporate Events

Corporate Foundations

Corporate Membership Packages

Correspondence

CPR

Credit Card Transactions

Credits

CRM Systems

Cross-Industry Marketing
  Efforts

Customer Assistance

Customer Care

Customer Loyalty

Customer Relations

Customer Service

Customer Support Environment

Customers

Daily Reports

Data Entry

Delivery Processes

Department Regulations

Design

Desserts

Develop and Maintain Client
  Relationships

Distributors

Diversity

Diversity of Professionals

Documentation

Drafts

Economies of Scale

Emergency Equipment

Emergency Evacuation Plan

Employee Performance

Employee Relationship
  Management

Employee Satisfaction

ERP Systems

Establish Rapport

Executive Guidelines

Existing Accounts

Facility Operations

Fast Food Industry

Field Inquiries

Field Support

Filing

Filing Invoices

Filing System

Filling Job Orders

Finance

Financial Experience

Financial Record Keeping

Financial Systems

Front Desk Operations

Front-End Systems

Guest Check In

Guest Check Out

Guest Complaints

Guest Mail and Faxes

Guest Rooms

Guest Services

Guest Survey

Guests' Needs

Guidelines

Hospitality Oriented

Human Resources

Incoming Calls

Increased Sales

Independent Worker

Instructions

Interpersonal Skills

Inventory

Job Applicants

Job Openings

Job Placement

Light Maintenance

List Management

Mailing Checks and Statements

Managed Care Industry

Management Reports

Management Systems

Marketing Initiatives

Marketing Office

Marketing Plans

Marketing Report

Marketing Strategies

Materials Costing Processes

Media Relations

Merchandising

Monitor

Monitored Payroll

Monitoring Delivery Personnel

Monthly Menu

Monthly Reports

Monthly Seminars

Multiple Accounts

Multiple Tasks

National Business Convention

New Associate Training Program

New Business Development

Office Operations

Office Responsibilities

Operational Deadlines

Operational Procedures

Operations

Ordering

Organization of Delivery
    Schedules

Outbound Calls

Overnight Operations

Passenger Boarding

Passenger Manifest

Passenger Safety

Passengers

Patient

Payroll

Performance

Performance Bonus

Personalized Client Interactions

Personnel

Personnel Assistance

Personnel Management

Phone Interaction

Plan Design Features

Plane Reservations

Portioning

Practical Applications

Premium Refund

Prep Work

Preparation

Pre-Selected Client Groups

Presentation

Presentation of Goods

Prioritize Tasks at Hand

Problem Area

Problem Resolution

Problem-Solving

Procedures

Process Payments

Processing Returns

Production

Products

Professional Image

Professional Services
  Environment

Promotion

Promotional Demonstration
  Activities

Promotional Efforts

Promotional Events

Promotional Opportunities

Prospective Customers

Proven Track Record

Public Relations

Purchasing

Purchasing Procedures

Quality Control

Quick and Accurate Decisions

Realization of Customer
  Specifications

Receiving

Reconciling

Reconciling Commission Reports

Referral Service

Referrals

Register Control

Registers

Relationship Building

Relationship Building Skills

Rentals

Reporting Tools

Reports

Requisitions

Researching and Resolving
  Customer Inquiries

Reservations

Resolve Customer Complaints

Resolve Guest Grievances/
  Problems

Restaurants

Retail

Route-Oriented Industry

Sales Goals

Sales Programs

Sales Staff

Sales Support Services

Sales Territory Development

Sales/Marketing

Schedule of Shows

Scheduling

Seating Allocation

Selection and Referral Process

Seminar

Service Business Systems

Service Distributors

Service Opportunities

Service Procedures

Services

Shift Management

Shift Scheduling

Shipping

Shipping Errors

Shop Management

Show Expenses

Sourcing Network

Sourcing of Vendors

Special Functions

Special Interest Groups

Special Orders

Special Sales

Specialized Training

Staff Motivation

Staff Training

Standardized Processes

Stations

Strong Academic Background

Strong Communication Skills

Supermarkets

Supplies

System Support

Take Out

Team Member

Telemarketing

Telephone Bookings

Telephone Survey

Telex Bookings

Terminations and Commission
    Assignments

Three Star Hotel

Time and Labor Solutions

Tour Arrangements

Tourist Information

Tracking Demands

Tradeshows

Training Program

Transactions

Transportation Coordination

Travel Problems

Troubleshoot

Typing

Weekly Volume

Weekly Work Schedule

Work Flow

Workshops

COMMONLY USED ACTION VERBS:

Arranged	Ensured	Prepared
Assisted	Evaluated	Provided
Conducted	Generated	Received
Demonstrated	Handled	Served
Designed	Ordered	Trained
Developed	Performed	Utilized

ACTION VERBS AND BUZZ WORDS USED IN CONTEXT:

• *Handled* cash intake, inventory control, and light maintenance.

• *Worked* directly with the executive pastry chef. *Monitored* the baking, mixing, and finishing of cakes, pastries, and a full range of bakery products.

• *Utilized* creative talents to develop *attractive presentations*; *demonstrated* original ideas.

• *Showed* expertise and accuracy with *pre-flight procedures*; *ensured* the safety and comfort of all passengers. Knowledge of *CPR/First Aid* if necessary.

• *Worked* as *certified flight attendant* with over four years experience working *overseas/domestic flights*.

• *Implemented* comprehensive Health/Fitness Evaluation, incorporating components of *strength, flexibility, cardiovascular/muscular endurance*, and *cardiac risk factors*.

• *Made* restaurant *recommendations* and dinner *reservations* based on comprehensive knowledge and contact with area restaurants and management.

CHAPTER TWENTY-SEVEN

SOCIAL AND HUMAN SERVICES

INDUSTRY BUZZ WORDS FOR these helping fields highlight experience with improving the emotional well-being of individuals in need; studying human behavior and mental processes to understand, explain, and change people's behavior; developing programs to provide for growth and revitalization of urban, suburban, and rural communities and their regions; and helping local officials make decisions on social, economic, and environmental problems. This also includes work in group homes and halfway houses, correctional, mental retardation, and community mental health centers.

COMMON POSITIONS INCLUDE:

Case Manager	Program Coordinator
Case Worker	Program Director
Counselor	Psychiatric Counselor
Economic Development	Psychologist
Coordinator	Social Worker
Human Services Worker	Therapist
Legal Advocate	Urban Planner

RESUME BUZZ WORDS:

24-Hour Hotline

Academic Assistance

Achievement Test

Administrative Duties

Admissions

Adoption Purposes

Advocacy

After-School Program

Assessment of Clientele

Assignment of Children

Assisted Living

At Risk Students

Behavior Modification

Behavioral Programs

Bicultural Experience

Bilingual

Campaign Fund Solicitations

Case Management

Case Presentations

Case Prevention

Case Studies

Child Advocate

Clarification Exercise

Client Need

Client Progress

Clientele

Clients

Clinical

Clinical Practices

Clinical Treatment Plans

Co-Directed

College-Prep Test

Commercial Development

Community Agencies

Community Development Group

Community Group Meetings

Community Mobilization

Community Outreach

Community Residents

Community-Based Agencies

Compliance

Concrete and Supportive Services

Conduct Assessment

Consultant Reports

Contact Development

Content Planning

Cooperative Experience

Counseling

Credit Management

Credit Program

Crisis Intervention

Crisis Situation

Curriculum Development

Curriculum Implementation

Curriculum Recommendations

Daily Living Skills

Department of Social Services
(DSS)

Developmental Stimulation

Developmentally Delayed Clients

Diagnostic Evaluation

Difficult-to-Place Clients

Direct Assistance

Direct Patient Care

Discharge Planning

Disciplinary Problems

Discipline

Discussion Groups

Economic Analysis

Economic Development

Editorial Department

Education

Education for Families

Educational Institutes

Educational Testing

Effective Treatment Strategies

Efficient Daily Operations

Emotional Support

Enterprise Project

Evaluation of Mental Status

Extrinsic Motivation

Families at Risk

Families in Crisis

Family Life Education Group

Family Therapy

Feasibility Analysis

Foundation Fundraising

Fund Raising

Grant Programs

Grant Proposals

Group Activities

Group Practice

Group Therapy Sessions

Home Studies

Hot Line Calls

House Management

Housing Authority

Housing Development

Human Services

Hypothesis Testing

Individual Educational Programs

Individual Psychotherapy
    Sessions

Individual Social Work

Individualized Academic
    Instruction

Industrial Expansion

Industrial Retention

Informal Family Therapy

Information Referral

Initial Evaluation

In-Service Education

In-Service Training

Interdisciplinary Team

Intrinsic Motivation

Knowledge Management

Legal Resources

Legislative Documents

Local Organizations

Long-Term Treatment Plans

Maintenance Services

Managed Cases

Management Development

Mass Mailing Programs

Medical Charts

Multidisciplinary Education

Multidisciplinary Team

Negotiation

New Programs

Nonprofit Organization

Nursing Care

On-Call

One-on-One Meetings

One-to-One Basis

Outpatient Clinic

Outpatients

Outreach Clinical Services

Outreach Services

Outside Consulting

Parent Education Groups

Parent-Teacher Conferences

Patient Independence

Personal Practice

Petitions

Placement Services

Play Groups

Policies and Procedures

Policy Development

Position Case Study

Preventive Strategies

Primary Care

Private Agencies

Private Practice

Problem Diagnosis

Procedural Guidelines

Professional Development

Progress Charting

Project Development

Promotional Letters

Proposals

Protective Custody

Psychiatric Admissions

Psychiatric Assessment

Psychological Assistance

Psychological Testing

Public Agencies

Public Relations

Record Keeping System

Records

Recreation

Recruitment

Recruitment of Prospective
    Parents

Referral Requests

Referral Services

Regression Analysis

Relationship of Trust

Remedial Plans

Residential Program

Residential Treatment Facility

Routine Monitoring

Self-Image Enhancement

Seminars

Service Networks

Shelter

Situation Evaluation

Skill Utilization

Small Scale Enterprise

Social Assistance

Social Problems

Social Service Arena

Social Service Organization

Social Work

Special Service Network

Specialized Services

Status Reports

Students

Survival Skills

Task Force

Teaching Staff

Technical Assistance

Therapeutic Activities

Therapeutic Intervention

Therapeutic Plans

Treatment

Treatment Plans

Vocational Test

Work Flow

Workshops

Youth Programs

COMMONLY USED ACTION VERBS:

Administered

Assessed

Assisted

Coordinated

Counseled

Established

Evaluated

Handled

Initiated

Led

Managed

Observed

Organized

Provided

Responded

Reviewed

Served

Specialized

Streamlined

Taught

Treated

Worked

ACTION VERBS AND BUZZ WORDS USED IN CONTEXT:

- *Established* trusting relationships with individuals; accurately *kept records*; positively *related* with people from *diverse backgrounds*.

- *Coordinated* *administrative duties* for *after-school*

program and *served* as *liaison* between department and teaching staff.

• *Worked* with teachers in *preventive strategies* for *social disciplinary problems*.

• *Assessed* and *developed clinical treatment plans*; facilitated *crisis intervention procedures* and informal *family therapy*.

• *Initiated* and *developed* contacts with *political contributors* for conservative parties and organizations.

• *Provided crisis intervention* for both adults and adolescent clients; *handled psychiatric assessments* and *evaluations* and patient admission to specific unit. *Managed* and *stabilized unit teams* in resolving problems.

• *Oversaw foundation fundraising*, public relations, and information referral. *Assisted* in project development, implementation, and administration. *Organized* training programs for board and staff.

• *Administered psychological* and *educational testing* for students ranging from pre-kindergarten to fifth grade.

• *Worked* as a temporary substitute in a variety of *human service programs* including supervising adolescents in *group homes* and substitute teaching at institutions.

• *Tracked abuse/neglect cases* to ensure that *status reports and petitions* were filed accurately and on time.

• *Reorganized* administrative structure; *developed* policies and procedures; *wrote* new *policy manual*.

CHAPTER TWENTY-EIGHT

TECHNICAL

TECHNICAL INDUSTRY BUZZ

words highlight experience with applying specialized knowledge of technology, systems, engineering, and science. Potential applications for technical skills and experience exist in virtually all industries, including transportation, building design and inspection, engine repair and maintenance, electrical systems design, and communications.

COMMON POSITIONS INCLUDE:

Aircraft Pilot

Architect

Broadcast Technician

Building Inspector

Drafter

Electrician

Electronic Equipment Repairer

Engineering Technician

Landscape Architect

Mechanic

Millwright

Precision Inspector

QA Test Technician

Quality Control Inspector

Research and Development Technician

Surveyor

Technical Illustrator

Technical Instructor

Technical Support Specialist

Technical Writer

Telecommunications Consultant

RESUME BUZZ WORDS:

Administration Lead
Air-Cooled Condenser
Aircraft Maintenance
Aircraft Power
Aircraft Towing
Alignment
Analog
Analytical Attributes
Annual Network Costs
Architectural Development
Architectural Landscape
    Design
Architectural Landscaping
Architectural Renderings
Architecture
Artistic Illustration
Assemble
Assembly Drawing
Attainment
Baffle Tiles
Battery Connections
Battery Disconnections
Blueprints
Boiler Hookup
Boilers
Bookkeeping
Building Codes
Building Inspection
Building Laws

Bulk Memory Cards
Burners
Cable Drawings
Calcium Silicate Block
Chart
Chimney
Civil Engineering
Codes and Standards
Commercial Buildings
Commercial Wiring
Commercials
Community Production
Completed Framing
Compliance Procedures
Component Drawing
Component Parts
Computer Aided
Computer Aided Design (CAD)
Computer Design Base (CDB)
Computer Product
Computer Programming
Computer Science
Computer Trade Show
Computer Work Station
Conceptualization Stage
Concrete Design
Condenser
Condenser Head
Configuration Time

Continuing Engineering Functions
Control Chart
Cost Control
Craft Workers
Custom Construction
Custom Style
Customer Housing
Customer Service
Customer Support
Cylinder
Data Testing Standards
Database
Database Management
Datum Structure
Design Development
Development
Diagnostic Test
Digital Concept
Dimensioning System
Dimmer Board
Disassemble
Disk Interface
Distributor
Drafting
Drafting Technology
Drawing
Drawing Development and Detailing
Electrical
Electrical Regulations

Electrical Repairs
Electrical Technology
Electronic
Electronic Illustration
Electronics Technology
Emissions Certificate
Engine Cowl
Engineering
Equipment Application
Estimate
Experience
Exploded View
Exterior
External Credentialing Groups
Extrusions
Fabricated Complex Parts
Fabrication
Facility Justification of Systems and Networks
Federal Licensing/Certification
Field Drawing
Field Service
Field Service Engineer
Field Tested
Film Production
Final Inspection
Final Product Design
Final Recommendation
Final Release
Final Report
Fire Brink

Flat Patterns

Flight Officer

Flight-Line Launching

Flight-Line Recoveries

Floating Point Processors

Floor Framing

Flow Model

Fluid System Design

Footings

Foreman

Fuel Product

General Construction

General Repairs

Grading Safety Laws

Graph

Hand Tools

Hardware

Harnessing

High-Speed Logic Board

Hybrid Microcircuit Design and
    Drawing

Illustration

Image Memory Cards

In Process

Incoming Material

Information Distribution

In-Plant

Inspection

Inspection Area

Inspection Records

Inspection Technique

Insulator Skills

Interfacing

Interior Spaces

Internal Support

Internal Technical Operations

International Broadcasting

International Marketing Tool

Interpret Legal Requirements

Inventory

Landing Gear

Lights

Line Artwork

Lock Repair

Lubrication

Machine and Sheet Metal Parts
    Inspection

Machine Drawing

Machine Language Firmware

Machined

Machinery Support

Mainframe

Maintenance

Manufactured Products

Manufacturing

Mason Skills

Mechanical

Mechanical Aptitude

Mechanical/Electronic Detailing
    and Drawing

Microcomputer Industry

Microprocessor Principles

Military Construction

Military Hardware

Model Assembly

Model Construction

Model Part

Multilocation Companies

Multimedia Product

Network Design

Network Facility

On-Site Research

Operating Systems

Operational Discrepancy Logs

Operations

Overlay Applications

Parts Numbering System

Permanent Building Inspector

Permits

Photo-Typesetting

Piping

Plant Construction

Plumbing Regulations

Precision Inspection

Presentation

Presentation Graphics

Pressure Chamber

Pressure Fuel Oil Tank

Pressure Parts

Preventive Maintenance

Print Specification

Private Sectors

Procedure

Product Development

Product Performance

Product Reliability

Production

Program Logs

Program Management
Techniques

Program Sources

Project Leadership

Project Management

Project Scheduling Priority
System

Project Superintendent

Promos

Proposal

Prototype System

Public Sectors

Public Service Announcements

Public Works

Pump

Quality Assurance

Quality Workmanship

Radio-Television-Film
Technology

Real Estate Development Layout

Reconfiguration

Refueling

Refurbished Technology

Regulations

Regulatory Compliances

Repair

Research

Research Data

Residential Electrical Needs

Residential Heating Needs

Residential Plumbing Needs

Residential Wiring

Retaining Walls

Revision Cycle

Routing Sheet

Sample Part

Sand Casting

Satellite Feeds

Schematic Capture

Scoop Lights

Service Manual

Servicing

Sheet Metal Drawing

Sheet Metal Layout Inspection

Sheet-Metal Fabrication

Single Location Companies

Site Survey

Software

Software Enhancements

Specifications

Stairway

Standards

State Building Codes

State Rules and Regulations

Station Organization

Strategic Alliance

Streamlined Procedures

Strict Quality Control

Structural Steel Work

Studio Camera

Studio System

Sub-Assembly

Submit Reports

Submittal

Successful Development

Surface Ship Propulsion System

System Design

System Recommendation

System Test

System Test Board

Tactical Research

Technical Drawing

Technical Illustration

Technical Writing

Telecommunications

Television Production

Template

Terminal

Territory Management

Test Date Format

Test Equipment

Test File

Test Results

Testing Program

Testing Time

Topographical Survey

Track Trends

Transmitter Logs

Troubleshooting

Turbines

Variances

Verbal Specification

Video Adjuster Boards

Video Conference

Video Latch Boards

Video Sync Boards

Well Developed

Wing Tips

Wiring

Wiring Lamps

Working Audit

Working Drawing

Workstation Product Lines

Worldwide Television
Deregulation

Writing Diagrams

Zoning Laws

Zoning Safety Laws

COMMONLY USED ACTION VERBS:

Assigned	Interpreted	Tested
Communicated	Modified	Trained
Conducted	Outlined	Updated
Created	Programmed	Used
Designed	Promoted	Utilized
Developed	Researched	Worked
Edited	Services	
Evaluated	Started	

ACTION VERBS AND BUZZ WORDS USED IN CONTEXT:

• *Trained* in *maintenance, servicing,* and *troubleshooting* on all areas of aircraft from *wing tips* to *landing gear,* nose to tail, interior and exterior, including removals and replacements of *component parts,* repairs, lubrications, refueling, and *flight-line launching and recoveries.*

• *Worked* within both the *public and private sectors.* Required knowledge of local government agency procedures (e.g., obtaining *permits, variances,* interfacing with the Building, Planning, and Engineering Departments).

• *Created* and *interpreted* *testing programs* to evaluate and modify *product performance* and *reliability* for manufacturer of commercial kitchen equipment.

• *Developed* standard designs for *retaining walls* and *reinforced-concrete* bridge abutments, the design of which are still currently being used.

• *Used* verbal *specifications* to develop *electronic illustrations* for new and changed products.

• *Researched* the effect of worldwide television *deregulation* on broadcast, cable and satellite television, as well as international broadcasting and advertising.

CHAPTER TWENTY-NINE

TRANSPORTATION AND TRAVEL

IN THE TRANSPORTATION AND travel industries, buzz words highlight experience with conveying passengers or goods, providing or controlling means for transportation, and coordinating or advancing the travel of others. They also include knowledge of various transportation methods, either from the customer service side or the transporting side.

COMMON POSITIONS INCLUDE:

Airline Reservation
　　Representative
Cargo Assistant
Coach Operator
Concierge
Corporate Travel Accountant
Dispatch Operator
Driver
Flight Attendant
Inbound Coordinator
Inspector

Passenger Service Agent
Pilot
Ticket Agent
Transit Driver
Transit Planner
Transportation Planning
　　Manager
Travel Agent
Travel Consultant
Trucker

RESUME BUZZ WORDS:

Air Compressor

Air Express Network

Air Freight

Air Tank

Aircraft

Aircraft Fittings

Airframe Services

Airport Code

Airport Facilities

Airport Transfers

Airports

Alignment

Area School Bus Company

Assembly

Automated Control Systems

Automated Guideway Transit

Automatic Train Control

Average Weekday Traffic

Aviation Industry

Baggage Check

Barges

Berthing Facilities

Boarding Pass

Boxcars

Brake Shoes

Bulk Freight Shipping

Bulk Transportation

Bus Service

Buses

Business Meetings

Business Trips

Cab Signaling Equipment

Cabin Cleaning

Cam Buckles

Canal System

Canopy Platform

Capacity

Capital Asset Financing

Car Maintenance

Car Rental Agreement

Car Repair

Cargo Handling

Cargo Restraint Equipment

Cargo Services

Carrier

Carry-On

Charter Bus Service

Charter Services

Chemicals

City-Funded

Cleaning Planes

Coal Cars

Code System Emulators

Commission

Commission Sales Agents

Commodities

Common Carrier Freight Line

Common Carrier Trucking Firm

Communities

Commuter Train Lines

Complete Packaged
  Transportation Service

Computerized Aircraft
  Maintenance Services

Confirmation

Connecting Flight

Connections

Constituent Agencies

Construction Aggregate

Construction Services

Container Freight Station
  Operations

Containerized Cargo
  Distribution System

Contracting Services

Control Systems

Corporate Clients

Corporate Rate

Covered Hoppers

Cruise Line

Cruise Speed

Customs Brokerage

Deep-Sea and Coastal Towing

Dinner/Theater Events

Direct Flight

Direct Services

Discount Fairs

Dispatch Computer

Distribution

Districts

Domestic Offices

Domestic Travel

Double Stack Intermodal
  Facilities

Drop-Off Locations

Dwell Time

Electronic Controls

Elements

Emergency Air and Truck Freight
  Services

Emergency Road Services

Engine Services

Engineering Consulting

Equipment Housings

Equipment Management Services

Executive Travel

Expedited Air and Truck Freight
  Services

Express Services

Express Transportation

Extensive Commuter Passenger
  Service Railroad Operations

Fare

Flat Rate

Fleet

Fleet Financing

Floor Jack

Foreign Travel

Freight Cars

Freight Forwarding

Freight Handling

Freight Service Railroad Operations

Freight Traffic

Fueling Planes

Full-Service

Global Transportation

Ground-Handling

Group Rate

Guideway

Heavy Rail Transit

High-Speed Rail

Highway Trailers

Highways

Household Goods

Import/Export Brokerage

Inbound Marine Shipping

Independent Contractors

Industrial Development

In-House Capabilities

Inspections

Insurance

Integrated Logistics Programs

Intermodal Cars

Intermodal Distribution Company

International Air and Ocean Freight Forwarding Services

International Air Carrier

International Travel

Interstate Freight Carrier

Into-Plane Fueling

Jumper Cables

Land Shippers

Lease Types

Leasing Company

Light Rail Transit

Limousine Transportation Services

Loading Standards

Loading/Unloading

Local Service

Lock-Out Tools

Locomotives

Logistics

Main Lines

Mainline Railways

Maintenance

Major Cities

Major Lessor

Major Markets

Marine Divisions

Marine Towing

Marine Transportation

Maritime Academies

Mass Transportation

Microprocessor-Based Automatic Train Control

Mileage

Modification Services

Motor Carrier

Motor Freight Carrier

Motorists

Shoring Beams

Sightseeing Activities

Signals

Spare Parts Inventory

Special Projects

Specialized Transportation
Services

Specialty Cars

Standby

Station

Steam Generators

Steel Products

Storage Services

Storage Tanks

Subways

Switch Machines

Switching Track

Tank Cars

Tank Storage Terminals

Terminal

Ticket Broker

Tire Iron

Tow Services

Track

Track Circuits

Tractors

Traditional Freight Forwarding

Transit Rails

Transportation Services

Travel

Travel Agency

Travel Demand

Trips

Trolleys

Truck Rental Company

Truck Transportation

Trucking

Trucking Company

Truckload Transportation Services

Tugs

Turnaround Time

Vacations

Van Transportation Company

Vehicle Leasing Companies

Vehicles

Vital Processors

Vital Timers

Volume

Warehouse Space

Warehousing

Warehousing Facilities

Wayside

Weddings

Wheel Services

Wheels

Winches

Work Equipment

Workstation-Based Systems

Worldwide Supply Chain
Solutions

Yachts

Yard Track

COMMONLY USED ACTION VERBS:

Conducted	Flew	Prepared
Confirmed	Handled	Programmed
Contacted	Instructed	Scheduled
Coordinated	Mapped	Sold
Drove	Operated	Transported
Enforced	Performed	Traveled
Filed	Planned	

ACTION VERBS AND BUZZ WORDS USED IN CONTEXT:

- *Planned vacations* and *business trips*, both *foreign* and *domestic*, for *discount service travel agency*.

- *Confirmed ticket purchases*, *scheduled connecting flights*, and *contacted transportation services* for passengers.

- *Mapped out route systems* for buses in coordination with *peak periods*.

- *Operated commuter rail*, adhering to all *mass transit* regulations.

- *Enforced safety policies and procedures* for *specialized vehicles*.

- *Sold passes* for *incoming* and *outgoing trains*, *handled* switching *track operations*, and was responsible for general managing of station.

- *Programmed self-propelled vehicles* and *self-unloading bulk carriers*; *performed maintenance* when necessary.

- *Coordinated* sightseeing activities, *made* restaurant *reservations*, and *arranged* other local services for *tourists*.

- *Drove* public *shuttle bus* on *express service route* with designated *drop-off locations*.

- *Filed* reports on *average weekly traffic* and *planned traffic routes* with fluctuating *rush hour schedules*.

CHAPTER THIRTY

VISUAL AND PERFORMING ARTS

THESE BUZZ WORDS FOR THE visual and performing arts concentrate on those positions for creative artists. (Chapter Six has more buzz words for those working in the arts and entertainment industries.) Arts buzz words highlight experience with creating art and with entertaining an audience through performance art, theater, and music. This includes organizing and designing articles, products, and materials; portraying people, places, and events; communicating ideas, thoughts, and feelings; making words come alive by creating a visual and oral presentation based on written words in a script; expressing ideas, stories, rhythm, and sound; and creating dance interpretations.

COMMON POSITIONS INCLUDE:

Actor/Actress	Commercial Artist/Instructor
Art Administrator	Conductor
Art Director	Co-Producer
Choreographer	Dancer
Comedian	Desktop Publisher

Fashion Designer

Film Production Assistant

Graphic Artist/Designer

Interior Designer

Model

Musician

Photographer

Production (Tour) Manager

Production Coordinator

Talent Agent

Theatrical Director

Visual Artist

RESUME BUZZ WORDS:

Accessory

Act

Advertising

Airbrush

Album Tour

Apparel

Architectural Design

Artist Shop

Artistic Feasibility

Artwork

Ballet

Black and White

Book Illustration

Bound Printed Material

Broadway

Brochures

Business and Art Professional

Cable Program

Calligraphic Artwork

Camera Ready Art

Charts

Choreography

Classical Ballet

Classical Piano

Color

Color Film Development

Color Promotional Samples

Comedy Sketch

Commercial Art

Commercials

Computer Art

Contemporary Ballet

Corporate Design

Corporate Portrait

Costume Design

Costumes

Creative Analysis

Creative Dance

Creative Planning

Dance Studio

Dealer Sell Sheets

Debut Album

Departmental Database Network

Design

Design Logos

Diagram

Diagram Maps

Direct Lighting

Display Technique

Drum Technician

Extra

Fabric

Fashion Design

Fashion Show

Fashion Tradeshow

Feature Film

Fine Arts

Flyers

Free-Standing Insert Ads

Freehand

Freelance

Front Window Display

Full Color

Gallery Logo

Garment

Hand-Design

Header Cards

Illustration

Improvisational Workshop

In the Round

Independent Record

Interior Design

Interior Finish

Japanese Motif Sketch Design

Jazz

Large Format View Camera

Laser Printing

Layout and Design

Lighting

Lighting Effects

Lighting Equipment

Location

Location Photography

Mail Marketing Pieces

Major Label

Makeup

Marketing Brochure

Marketing Lists

Material

Mechanical Paste-Up

Mechanical Stages

Mechanicals

Method Style of Acting

Model

Modern Ballet

Modern Dance

Modern Piece

Music Director

Music Format

Musical

Narrative Sketch

New York Stage

Onstage

Operational Deadlines

Orchestra

Orchestral Experience

Oriental Design

Outside Vendor

Pastels

Paste-Up

Pattern

Pattern Making

Performance

Performer

Photo Essay

Photography

Photography Sessions

Playwright's Text

Point-of-Sales Material

Portfolio

Portrait

Positive and Negative Images

Pre-Release

Printing

Printing Process

Producer

Production Report

Promotional Campaign

Promotional Event

Promotional Photography

Promotional Pieces

Promotions

Prop

Props and Backgrounds

Proscenium Arch

Prototype Design

Published

Radio Chart

Recital

Reprint Titles

Reproduction Camera

Road Crew

Road Tour

Runway Show

Scene

Script

Seasonal Floor Set

Set

Sew

Shelf Talkers

Showcase

Showcase Club

Sing

Sketch Comprehensives

Slide Materials

Slide Show

Small Format View Camera

Soft Sheets

Sound

Sound Technician

Sound Work

Special Effects

Special Market Division

Specialized Technology

Stage Direction

Stage Management

Staging

Stand-Up Comedy

Stanislavski Style of Acting

Stat Camera

Structure

Studio Art

Studio Assignment

Stylized Lettering

Superstructure

Tailor

Tap

Teaching

Tear-Off Pads

Technical Art

Technical Report

Theater Production

Theatrical Direction

Three Color Brochures

Tickets

Top 10 Selling Record

Trade Promotions

Traditional Art and Drawing

Traditional Painting and
   Drawing

Type Layout

Vendor

Video

Visual Audit

Visual Checklist

Visual Criteria Standardization

Visual Presentation

Wardrobe

Window Display

Window Display Fixture

Worldwide Tour

COMMONLY USED ACTION VERBS:

Achieved	Directed	Produced
Acted	Drew	Revised
Advertised	Focused	Sculpted
Assisted	Illustrated	Served
Built	Managed	Sewed
Choreographed	Organized	Shot
Communicated	Oversaw	Staged
Conceived	Painted	Videotaped
Coordinated	Performed	Worked
Created	Planned	Wrote
Designed	Played	

ACTION VERBS AND BUZZ WORDS USED IN CONTEXT:

- *Produced* *layout*, *paste-up*, and *mechanicals* of full-color, bound printed material.

- Successfully *planned*, *organized*, and *managed* studio specializing in *onstage dance* (*jazz, ballet, tap, modern* and *creative dance*).

- *Worked* in *artist shop* creating various *props* including tropical *set* for *disc jockey*. *Created* palm trees, *built* bamboo hut, and *integrated* *lighting effects* into structure/scene.

- *Videotaped* *improvisational workshop* for the L.A. Entertainment Theater, and *comedy sketches* for local talent.

- *Served* as *artistic support* for army base; *created flyers*, *charts*, *brochures*, *tickets*, *diagrams*, *maps*, and *design logos*.

- *Focused* on the physical requirements and restrictions of stages ranging from *in-the-round* to *proscenium arch*.

- *Co-produced* local *cable program*, showcasing a variety of *stand-up performers*.

- *Provided* tailoring, *wardrobe consultation*, and custom design of suits and evening wear.

PART TWO

POWERFUL WORDS
FOR EVERY RESUME

RESUME BUZZ WORDS

Assigned
Assisted
Assumed
Attained
Audite
Au

HOW YOU WRITE YOUR RESUME is just as important as what you write. In describing previous work experiences, the strongest resumes use short phrases beginning with action verbs and positive adverbs. Below are some of those you might want to use. These lists are not all-inclusive, but they should help you when you are trying to add variety and forcefulness to your descriptions of your job experiences and your abilities.

400 ACTION VERBS

Accelerated	Administered	Anticipated
Accentuated	Advanced	Applied
Accomplished	Advertised	Appointed
Achieved	Advised	Appraised
Acted	Advocated	Approved
Activated	Aided	Arbitrated
Actuated	Allocated	Arranged
Adapted	Amplified	Ascertained
Addressed	Analyzed	Assembled
Adjusted	Answered	Assessed

...gmented	Completed	Defined
Authorized	Composed	Delegated
Awarded	Computed	Delivered
Balanced	Conceived	Demonstrated
Began	Conceptualized	Described
Boosted	Condensed	Designated
Briefed	Conducted	Designed
Broadened	Conferred	Detected
Budgeted	Conserved	Determined
Built	Consolidated	Developed
Calculated	Constructed	Devised
Captured	Consulted	Diagnosed
Cataloged	Contacted	Diagrammed
Centralized	Continued	Directed
Chaired	Contracted	Discovered
Charted	Contributed	Dispatched
Checked	Controlled	Dispensed
Clarified	Convened	Displayed
Classified	Converted	Dissected
Coached	Conveyed	Distributed
Collaborated	Convinced	Diverted
Collected	Cooperated	Documented
Combined	Coordinated	Drafted
Communicated	Corresponded	Drew
Compared	Counseled	Earned
Compiled	Created	Edited
	Critiqued	Educated
	Cultivated	Effected
	Customized	Eliminated
	Debugged	Emphasized
	Decided	Employed

Encouraged	Formulated	Informed
Enforced	Fostered	Initiated
Engineered	Found	Innovated
Enhanced	Founded	Inspected
Enlarged	Fulfilled	Inspired
Enlisted	Furnished	Installed
Ensured	Gained	Instituted
Entered	Gathered	Instructed
Entertained	Generated	Integrated
Established	Governed	Interacted
Estimated	Grossed	Interpreted
Evaluated	Guided	Interviewed
Examined	Handled	Introduced
Executed	Harmonized	Invented
Expanded	Headed	Inventoried
Expedited	Heightened	Investigated
Experimented	Helped	Invited
Explained	Hired	Involved
Explored	Honed	Issued
Expressed	Hosted	Joined
Extended	Hypothesized	Judged
Extracted	Identified	Kept
Fabricated	Illustrated	Launched
Facilitated	Imagined	Learned
Fashioned	Implemented	Lectured
Filed	Improved	Led
Finalized	Improvised	Lifted
Fixed	Incorporated	Listened
Focused	Increased	Located
Forecasted	Indexed	Logged
Formed	Influenced	Maintained

Managed	Persuaded	Published
Manipulated	Photographed	Purchased
Marketed	Piloted	Qualified
Matched	Pinpointed	Questioned
Maximized	Pioneered	Raised
Measured	Placed	Ran
Mediated	Planned	Rated
Merged	Played	Reached
Mobilized	Posted	Realized
Modified	Predicted	Reasoned
Monitored	Prepared	Received
Motivated	Prescribed	Recommended
Navigated	Presented	Reconciled
Netted	Preserved	Recorded
Observed	Presided	Recruited
Obtained	Prevented	Reduced
Opened	Printed	Reestablished
Operated	Prioritized	Reevaluated
Orchestrated	Processed	Referred
Ordered	Produced	Regulated
Organized	Professionalized	Rehabilitated
Originated	Programmed	Reinforced
Outdid	Projected	Reinvigorated
Outlined	Promoted	Related
Overcame	Promulgated	Remodeled
Overhauled	Proofread	Rendered
Oversaw	Proposed	Reorganized
Paid	Protected	Repaired
Participated	Proved	Replaced
Passed	Provided	Reported
Performed	Publicized	Represented

Researched	Solved	Totaled
Reshaped	Sorted	Tracked
Resolved	Spearheaded	Traded
Responded	Specialized	Trained
Restored	Specified	Transcribed
Restructured	Spoke	Transformed
Resupplied	Sponsored	Translated
Retrieved	Staffed	Transmitted
Revamped	Standardized	Transported
Reviewed	Started	Traveled
Revised	Streamlined	Tutored
Revitalized	Strengthened	Uncovered
Routed	Structured	Undertook
Saved	Studied	Unified
Scheduled	Substituted	United
Screened	Suggested	Updated
Searched	Summarized	Upgraded
Secured	Supervised	Used
Selected	Supplied	Utilized
Separated	Supplemented	Validated
Served	Supported	Verbalized
Serviced	Surpassed	Verified
Settled	Surveyed	Vitalized
Shaped	Sustained	Volunteered
Shared	Synthesized	Weighed
Signed	Systemized	Widened
Simplified	Targeted	Won
Simulated	Taught	Worked
Sketched	Terminated	Wrote
Sold	Tested	
Solicited	Tightened	

400 ADVERBS

Absolutely
Accommodatingly
Accordingly
Accurately
Actively
Acutely
Adamantly
Adeptly
Adequately
Adroitly
Advantageously
Affably
Affectingly
Affectionately
Affirmatively
Aggressively
Alertly
Ambitiously
Amicably
Amply
Analytically
Appraisingly
Appreciatively
Appropriately
Artfully
Articulately
Artistically
Assertively
Assuredly

Astutely
Attentively
Authoritatively
Automatically
Autonomously
Avidly
Beamingly
Beautifully
Becomingly
Befittingly
Believably
Bravely
Brightly
Brilliantly
Busily
Calmly
Candidly
Capably
Carefully
Caringly
Casually
Cautiously
Ceremoniously
Charmingly
Cheerfully
Cheerily
Civilly
Cleanly
Cleverly

Closely
Coherently
Colorfully
Comfortably
Comfortingly
Commandingly
Communicatively
Comparatively
Competently
Competitively
Completely
Composedly
Comprehendingly
Concisely
Conclusively
Confidentially
Confidently
Congenially
Conscientiously
Consciously
Conservatively
Consistently
Conveniently
Convincingly
Coolly
Cooperatively
Cordially
Correctively
Courageously

Courteously	Effectively	Fondly
Creatively	Effervescently	Forcefully
Critically	Efficiently	Forcibly
Decidedly	Effortlessly	Foresightedly
Decisively	Elaborately	Formally
Definitely	Elegantly	Frankly
Deftly	Eloquently	Freely
Deliberately	Emphatically	Freshly
Delicately	Encouragingly	Gaily
Delightedly	Energetically	Gallantly
Delightfully	Engagingly	Gamely
Demonstrably	Enjoyably	Generously
Dependably	Enthusiastically	Genially
Descriptively	Evenly	Gently
Determinedly	Exactingly	Genuinely
Devotedly	Experimentally	Gleefully
Dexterously	Expertly	Good-Naturedly
Dignifiedly	Explicitly	Gracefully
Diligently	Expressively	Graciously
Diplomatically	Extensively	Gradually
Directly	Exuberantly	Grammatically
Discreetly	Faithfully	Gratefully
Distinctly	Favorably	Handily
Divinely	Fearlessly	Happily
Doggedly	Fervently	Harmoniously
Dramatically	Fiercely	Heartily
Drastically	Firmly	Heedfully
Eagerly	Fittingly	Helpfully
Earnestly	Flexibly	Honestly
Easily	Fluently	Honorably
Educationally	Fluidly	Hopefully

Hopingly	Judiciously	Observantly
Humbly	Justly	Occasionally
Imaginatively	Keenly	Officially
Immaculately	Kindly	Openly
Independently	Knowingly	Optimistically
Indirectly	Laboriously	Outrageously
Industriously	Liberally	Overwhelmingly
Informatively	Lightly	Painstakingly
Ingeniously	Logically	Particularly
Inquisitively	Loyally	Passionately
Insightfully	Lucidly	Patiently
Insistently	Mannerly	Peacefully
Instinctively	Masterfully	Perceptively
Instinctually	Maturely	Perfectly
Instructively	Meaningfully	Perkily
Intellectually	Mechanically	Perpetually
Intelligently	Merrily	Perseveringly
Intelligibly	Methodically	Persistently
Intensely	Meticulously	Persuasively
Intently	Mindfully	Physically
Interestedly	Minutely	Plainly
Intrepidly	Moderately	Playfully
Intricately	Modestly	Pleasantly
Intriguingly	Naturally	Pleasingly
Intuitively	Neatly	Pointedly
Inventively	Nicely	Politely
Jauntily	Nimbly	Positively
Jocularly	Nobly	Potently
Jointly	Noncompetitively	Practically
Jovially	Obediently	Precisely
Joyfully	Obligingly	Preparedly

Professionally	Robustly	Stately
Proficiently	Routinely	Steadfastly
Profoundly	Satisfactorily	Steadily
Progressively	Securely	Stoutly
Promptly	Selectively	Straightforwardly
Properly	Self-Assuredly	Strategically
Proudly	Selflessly	Strictly
Prudently	Sensibly	Strongly
Punctiliously	Sensitively	Studiously
Purposefully	Seriously	Stupendously
Quickly	Sharply	Sturdily
Rapidly	Shrewdly	Stylishly
Rationally	Significantly	Substantially
Readily	Silently	Successfully
Realistically	Simply	Superbly
Reasonably	Simultaneously	Supportively
Reassuringly	Sincerely	Surely
Receptively	Single-Handedly	Sympathetically
Reflectively	Skillfully	Systematically
Refreshingly	Smartly	Tactfully
Regularly	Smoothly	Tastefully
Reliably	Snappily	Technically
Repeatedly	Solidly	Tenaciously
Resolutely	Soothingly	Thoroughly
Resoundingly	Sophisticatedly	Thoughtfully
Resourcefully	Soundly	Tirelessly
Respectably	Sparingly	Tolerantly
Respectfully	Spiritedly	Tremendously
Responsibly	Splendidly	Triumphantly
Responsively	Spontaneously	Trustingly
Rigorously	Stalwartly	Trustworthily

Truthfully
Unabashedly
Unaffectedly
Unassumingly
Unblinkingly
Uncritically
Understandingly
Unemotionally
Unequivocally
Unfalteringly
Unflinchingly
Unselfishly

Unsettlingly
Unusually
Unwaveringly
Unyieldingly
Uprightly
Urgently
Usefully
Valiantly
Valorously
Verbally
Vibrantly
Victoriously

Vigilantly
Vigorously
Voraciously
Warmly
Watchfully
Welcomingly
Wholeheartedly
Willfully
Willingly
Wisely
Zealously
Zestfully

CHAPTER THIRTY-TWO

DESIRABLE TRAITS FOR POTENTIAL EMPLOYEES

WHETHER YOU'RE APPLYING for a position in the travel industry or for a position in health care, there are certain professional characteristics and personality traits all employers look favorably upon. Below is a list of some of the more valuable traits and characteristics you'll want to showcase on your resume.

60 POSITIVE JOB-RELATED TRAITS

Analytical Skills	Dedicated
Articulate	Detail-Oriented
Attention to Detail	Determined
Capable	Diligent
Commitment to Service	Diplomatic
Common Sense	Driven
Communication Skills	Efficient
Computer Savvy	Energetic
Creative Thinker	Enthusiastic
Customer-Service-Oriented	Flexible
Decisive	Friendly

Goal-Oriented
Hard Worker
High Energy
Honest
Interpersonal Skills
Invested
Listening Skills
Managerial Abilities
Motivated
Negotiating Skills
Oral and Written
    Communications Skills
Organizational Skills
Outgoing
Patient
Poised
Positive Attitude
Problem Analysis Skills
Problem Solving Skills
Professional Appearance and
    Attitude

Prompt
Punctual
Quick Learner
Reliable Under Pressure
Resourceful
Responsible
Self-Motivated
Speaking Skills
Strategic Thinking
Strong Observational Skills
Team Player
Technical Skills
Time Management Skills
Trustworthy
Willing to Relocate
Willing to Travel
Word Processing Skills
Work Independently
Work Well Under Pressure

PART THREE

A HANDBOOK
FOR JOBSEEKERS

Part Three

CHAPTER THIRTY-THREE

RESUMES AND COVER LETTERS

WHEN FILLING A POSITION, an employer will often have 100-plus applicants, but time enough to interview only a handful of the most promising ones. As a result, he or she will reject most applicants after only briefly skimming their resumes.

Unless you have phoned and talked to the employer—which you should do whenever you can—you will be chosen or rejected for an interview entirely on the basis of your resume and cover letter. Your cover letter must catch the employer's attention, and your resume must hold it. But remember: A resume on its own is no substitute for an aggressive job search campaign. You must actively seek a job, and your resume is only one tool—albeit a critical one.

RESUME FORMAT: THE MECHANICS OF A GOOD FIRST IMPRESSION

Before even reading the words on your resume, a potential employer will begin to form an opinion of it—and, more importantly, of *you*—based on its format. No matter how good content it includes, a resume that is the wrong length, poorly organized, or difficult to read will have little chance of achieving its goal: getting you a job interview.

The Basics

Employers dislike long resumes, so unless you have an unusually strong background with many years of experience and a diversity of outstanding achievements, keep your resume length to one page. If you must squeeze in more information than would otherwise fit, try using a smaller typeface or changing the margins. With some word processing programs, you can decrease the font size of your paragraph returns and change the spacing between lines. Another way to cut the length of your resume is to look for paragraphs that end with lines of only one or two words; you can often free up space if you can shorten the information enough to get rid of those extra lines.

First impressions matter, so make sure the recruiter's first impression of your resume is a good one. Never handwrite your resume (or cover letter)! You should print your resume on standard 8½" x 11" paper. Recruiters often get resumes in batches of hundreds, and a smaller-sized resume may be lost in the pile. Oversized resumes are likely to get crumpled at the edges and won't fit easily into file folders.

You should print your resume on quality paper that has weight (24-pound weight is usual) and texture, in a conservative color such as white, ivory, or pale gray. Good resume paper is easy to find at many stores that sell stationery or office products. It is even available at some drugstores. Use matching paper and envelopes for both your resume and cover letter. One hiring manager at a major magazine throws out all resumes that arrive on paper that differs in color from the envelope!

Hiring someone for a job is serious business, so don't buy paper with images of clouds and rainbows in the background or anything that looks like casual stationery that you would send to your favorite aunt. You may want to include a personal touch, but don't spray perfume or cologne on your resume. Also, you shouldn't include your picture with your resume unless you have a specific and appropriate reason to do so.

Another tip: Be sure to do a test print of your resume (and cover letter) to make sure the watermark is on the same side as the text so that you can read it. Also make sure it is right-side up. As trivial as this may sound, some recruiters check for this! One recruiter at a law firm in New Hampshire sheepishly admitted this is the first thing he checks. "I open each envelope and check the watermarks on the resume and cover letter. Those candidates that have it wrong go into a different pile."

Getting It on Paper

A computer with a word processing or desktop publishing program is the most common way to generate your resume. This allows you the flexibility to make changes almost instantly and to store different drafts on disk. Word processing and desktop publishing programs also offer many different fonts to choose from, each taking up different amounts of space. (With the possible exception of some headings such as your name at the top, the text of a resume should generally stay between 10-point and 12-point font size.) Many other options are also available, such as boldfacing or italicizing for emphasis and the ability to change and manipulate spacing.

It is generally recommended to leave the right-hand margin unjustified as this keeps the spacing between the words even and is therefore easier to read.

For a resume on paper, the end result will be largely determined by the quality of the printer you use. Laser printers provide the best quality, though ink jet printers are also acceptable. Do not use a dot matrix printer.

Many companies now use scanning equipment to screen the resumes they receive, and certain paper, fonts, and other features are more compatible with this technology. White paper is preferable, as well as a standard font such as Courier or Helvetica. For a resume that will be scanned, you should use at least a 10-point font, and avoid using boldface, italics, underlining, borders, boxes, or graphics.

Household typewriters and office typewriters with nylon or other cloth ribbons are not good enough for typing your resume. If you don't have access to a quality word processing program, hire a professional with the resources to prepare your resume for you. Keep in mind that businesses such as Kinko's (which are often open 24 hours) provide access to computers with quality printers.

Even though it may look like an easy way to save time and money, don't make your copies on an office photocopier. Only the human resources office may see the actual resume you mail. Everyone else may see only a copy of it, and copies of copies quickly become unreadable. Furthermore, sending photocopies of your resume or cover letter is completely unprofessional. Either print out each copy individually, or take your resume to a professional copy shop, which will generally offer professionally maintained, extra-high-quality photocopiers and charge fairly reasonable prices. You want your resume to have a look of polished quality that represents you as best as possible.

Proof with Care

Whether you typed it yourself or paid to have it produced professionally, mistakes on resumes are not only embarrassing, but will also usually remove you from consideration. So proofread it as carefully as possible. Get a friend to help you, and read your draft aloud as your friend checks the proof copy. Then have your friend read aloud while you check. Next, read it letter by letter to check spelling and punctuation. One proofreading trick is to read your resume backwards, from the bottom up, as mistakes are often much more apparent if you're not reading the words in the same order you've seen a number of times before.

If you are having your resume typed or typeset by a resume service or a printer, and you don't have time to proof it, pay for it and take it home. Proof it there and bring it back later to get it corrected and printed.

When you write your resume with a word processing program, you can use the built-in spell checker to double-check for spelling errors. But keep in mind that a spell checker will not find errors such as "to" for "two" or "wok" for "work." Many spell-check programs also don't recognize missing or misused punctuation, nor are they set to check the spelling of capitalized words. It's important that you still proofread your resume to check for grammatical mistakes and other problems, even after it has been spellchecked. And if you do find mistakes, don't make edits in pen or pencil or use whiteout to fix them on the final copy! For a professional appearance, you'll have to print or type out the entire resume again.

ELECTRONIC RESUMES:
AN INCREASINGLY ESSENTIAL TOOL

As companies rely more and more on new technologies to find qualified candidates for job openings, you may find it worthwhile to create an electronic resume as well as a paper one. Why is this important? Companies today sometimes request that resumes be submitted by e-mail, and many hiring managers regularly check online resume databases for candidates to fill unadvertised job openings. Other companies enlist the services of electronic employment database services, which charge jobseekers a nominal fee to have their resumes posted to the database to be viewed by potential employers. Still other companies use their own automated applicant tracking systems, in which case your resume is fed through a scanner that sends the image to a computer that "reads" your resume, looking for keywords, and files it accordingly in its database.

Converting Your Resume

Whether you're posting your resume online, e-mailing it directly to an employer, sending it to an electronic employment database, or sending it to a company you suspect uses an automated applicant tracking system, you must create some form of electronic resume to even be considered. Don't panic! An electronic resume is simply a modified version of your conventional resume. Electronic resumes are generally sparsely formatted, but to be effective, they must be filled with keywords and important facts.

In order to post your resume to the Internet—either to an online resume database or through direct e-mail to an employer—you will need to change the way your resume is formatted. Instead of a Word, WordPerfect, or other word processing document, save your resume as a plain text, DOS, or ASCII file. These three terms are basically interchangeable, and they describe text at its simplest, most basic level, without the formatting such as boldface or italics that most jobseekers use to make their resumes look more interesting. If you use e-mail, you may have noticed that all of your messages are written and received in this format.

The first step in converting a resume from a conventional to electronic format is to remove all formatting from your resume including boldface, italics, underlining, bullets, differing font sizes, and graphics. Then, convert and save your resume as a plain text file. Most word processing programs have a "save as" feature that allows you to save files in different formats. Here, you should choose "text only" or "plain text."

Another option is to create a resume in HTML (hypertext markup language), the text formatting language used to publish information on the World Wide Web. However, the real usefulness of HTML resumes is still being explored. Most of the major online databases do not accept HTML resumes, and the vast majority of companies only accept plain text resumes through their e-mail.

The Value of Keywords

If you simply wish to send your resume to an electronic employment database or a company that scans resumes for an automated applicant tracking system, there is no need to convert your resume to a plain text file. The only change you need to make is to organize the information in your resume by keywords.

This is one way in which using some of the many buzz words given throughout this book becomes important. Employers are likely to do keyword searches for information, such as degree held or knowledge of particular types of software. Therefore, using the right keywords or key phrases in your resume is critical to its ultimate success. Keywords are usually nouns or short phrases that the computer searches for which refer to experience, training, skills, and abilities. For example, let's say an employer searches an employment database for a sales representative with the following criteria:

- BS/BA

- Exceeded Quota

- Cold Calls

- High Energy

- Willing to Travel

Even if you have the right qualifications, neglecting to use these keywords would result in the computer passing over your resume. Although there is no way to know for sure which keywords employers are most likely to search for, you can make educated guesses by checking the help-wanted ads or online job postings for your type of job. You should also arrange keywords in a keyword summary, a paragraph listing your qualifications that immediately follows your name and address. In addition, choose a nondecorative font with clear, distinct characters, such as Helvetica or Times. It is more difficult for a scanner to accurately pick up the more unusual fonts. Boldface and all capital letters are best used only for major section headings, such as "Experience" and "Education." It is also best to avoid using italics or underlining, since this can cause the letters to bleed into one another.

For more specific information on creating and sending electronic resumes, see *The Adams Internet Job Search Almanac*.

ORGANIZING YOUR RESUME: POSSIBLE FORMATS

Depending on which type of job you are seeking and which of your qualities and experiences you want to emphasize, you can organize your resume in several different ways. The most common resume formats are the functional resume, the chronological resume, and the combination resume.

A *functional* resume focuses on skills and de-emphasizes job titles, employers, and so forth. A functional resume is best if you have been out of the work force for a long time or are changing careers. It is also good if you want to highlight specific skills and strengths, especially if all of your work experience has been at one company. This format can also be a good choice if you are just out of school or have no experience in your desired field.

You may want to choose a *chronological* format if you are currently working or were working recently and if your most recent experiences relate to your desired field. Use reverse chronological order and include dates. To a recruiter, your last job and your latest schooling are the most important, so put the last first and list the rest going back in time.

A *combination* resume simply combines elements of the functional and chronological resume formats. This type of resume is used by many jobseekers who have a current position and a solid track record and who find elements from both types to be useful.

Contact Information

No matter which format you choose, your name, phone number, e-mail address (if you have one), and a complete mailing address should be at the top of your resume. Try to make your name stand out by using a slightly larger font size or all capital letters. Be sure to spell out everything. Never abbreviate St. for Street or Rd. for Road. If you are a college student, you should also put your home address and phone number at the top. Whatever phone number you use, you may find that you will need to change your message on your answering machine. Loud music in the background, a joke message that your friends find hilarious, or a message that doesn't include your actual name—these might all cause recruiters to reconsider their call and decide that they might not be interested in talking with you further.

Remember that employers will keep your resume on file and may contact you months later if a position opens that fits your qualifications. All too often, candidates are unreachable because they have moved and had not previously provided enough contact options on their resume. If you think you may be moving within six months, include a second address and phone number of a trusted friend or relative who can reach you no matter where you are.

Sections on Experience and Education

After your contact information, list your experience, then your education. If you are a recent graduate, list your education first, unless your experience is more important than your education. (For example, if you have just graduated from a teaching school, have some business experience, and are applying for a job in business, you would list your business experience first.)

Make sure that you make everything easy to find. In general, you should put the dates of your employment and education on the left of the page. For instance, put the names of the companies you worked for and the schools you attended a few spaces to the right of the dates. Then put the city and state or the city and country where you studied or worked to the right of the page.

The most important thing is simply to break up the text in some logical way that makes your resume visually attractive and easy to scan, so experiment to see which layout works best for your resume. However you set it up, stay consistent. Inconsistencies in fonts, spacing, or tenses will make your resume look sloppy. Also, be sure to use tabs to keep your information vertically lined up, rather than the less precise space bar.

RESUME CONTENT: SELLING YOURSELF

All of this talk about formatting, paper stock, fonts, and so on is fine, you may be saying to yourself, but what should I actually *write* in my resume? When you're composing the entries in your resume, always keep these two goals in mind:

1. Say It with Style   2. Sell Yourself

You are selling your skills and accomplishments in your resume, so it is important to inventory yourself and know yourself. If you have achieved something, say so.

Put it in the best possible light, but avoid subjective statements, such as "I am a hard worker" or "I get along well with my co-workers." Just stick to the facts.

While you shouldn't hold back or be modest, don't exaggerate your achievements to the point of misrepresentation. Be honest. Many companies will immediately drop an applicant from consideration (and may even fire a current employee) upon discovering inaccurate or untrue information on a resume or other application material.

You should certainly write down the all-important (and pertinent) things you have done, but do it in as few words as possible. Your resume will be scanned, not read, and short, concise phrases are much more effective than long-winded sentences. Avoid the use of "I" when emphasizing your accomplishments. Instead, use brief phrases beginning with action verbs.

While some technical terms will be unavoidable, you should try to avoid excessive "technicalese." Keep in mind that the first person to see your resume may be a human resources person who won't necessarily know all the jargon—and how can he or she be impressed by something incomprehensible?

Also, try to hold your paragraphs to six lines or fewer. If you have more than six lines of information about one job or school, put it in two or more paragraphs. A short resume will be examined more carefully. Remember: Your resume usually has between 8 and 45 seconds to catch an employer's eye. So make every second count.

Job Objectives

A functional resume may require a job objective to give it focus. A single phrase—or, at most, one or two sentences—describing the job you are seeking can clarify how you feel your skills will be best put to use. Be sure that your stated objective is in line with the position you're applying for.

Some examples of objectives:

- An entry-level editorial assistant position in the publishing industry.

- A senior management position with a telecommunications firm.

Don't include a job objective on a chronological resume unless your previous work experiences are completely unrelated to the position for which you're applying. An overly specific job objective might eliminate you from consideration for other positions that a recruiter feels are a better match for your qualifications. But even if you don't put an objective on paper, having a career goal in mind as you write can help give your entire resume a solid sense of direction.

Some jobseekers may choose to include both "Relevant Experience" and "Additional Experience" sections. This can be useful, as it allows you to place more emphasis on certain experiences and to de-emphasize others.

Presenting Your Experience

You should emphasize your continued experience in a particular job area or continued interest in a particular industry while de-emphasizing irrelevant positions. It is okay to include one opening line providing a general description of each company you've worked at. Delete positions that you held for less than four months (unless you are a very recent college grad or still in school). Stress your results and your achievements, elaborating on how you contributed in your previous jobs. Did you increase sales, reduce costs, improve a product, implement a new program? Were you promoted? Use specific numbers (i.e., quantities, percentages, dollar amounts) whenever possible.

Detailing Your Education

You should keep the education section of your resume brief if you have more than two years of career experience, though you may want to elaborate it more if you have less experience. If you are a recent college graduate, you may choose to include any high school activities that are directly relevant to your career. Once you are out of school for a while, you don't need to list your education prior to college.

This section should include degrees received and any honors or special awards. You might want to note individual courses or projects you participated in that would be relevant for employers. For example, if you are an English major applying for a position as a business writer, be sure to mention any business or economics courses. Previous experience such as Editor-in-Chief of the school newspaper would be relevant as well.

Highlight Impressive Skills

Be sure to mention any computer skills you may have. You may wish to include a section entitled "Additional Skills" or "Computer Skills," in which you list any software programs you have worked with. An additional skills section is also an ideal place to mention fluency in a foreign language.

If you are uploading your resume to an online job-hunting site, action verbs are still important, but the key words or key nouns that a computer would search for become more important. For example, if you're seeking an accounting position, key nouns that a computer would search for such as "spreadsheets" or "CPA" or "payroll" become very important.

Personal Data

This section is optional, but if you choose to include it, keep it brief. A one-word mention of hobbies such as fishing, chess, baseball, cooking, and so forth can give the person who will interview you a good way to open the conversation.

Team sports experience is looked at favorably. It doesn't hurt to include activities and interests that are somewhat unusual (fencing, Akido, '70s music) or that somehow relate to the position or the company to which you're applying. For instance, it would be worth noting if you are a member of a professional organization in your industry of interest. Never include information about your age, alias, date of birth, health, physical characteristics, marital status, religious affiliation, or political/moral beliefs.

References

For references, the most that is needed is the sentence "References available upon request" at the bottom of your resume. If you choose to leave it out, that's fine. This line is not really necessary. It is understood that references will most likely be asked for and provided by you later on in the interviewing process. Do not actually send references with your resume and cover letter unless specifically requested.

PROFESSIONAL RESUME WRITERS: GETTING HELP

If you can write reasonably well, it is to your advantage to write your own resume. Writing your resume forces you to review your experiences and figure out how to explain your accomplishments in clear, brief phrases. This will help you when you explain your abilities and work experience to interviewers. It is also easier to tailor your resume to each position you're applying for when you have put it together yourself.

If you write your resume, everything will be in your own words. It will sound like you; it will say what you want it to say. If you are a good writer, know yourself well, and have a good idea of which parts of your background employers are looking for, you should be able to write your own resume better than someone else. If you decide to write your resume yourself, have as many people as possible review and proofread it. Always be ready to welcome objective opinions and other perspectives.

When to Hire a Writer

If you have difficulty writing in "resume style" (which is quite unlike normal written language), if you are unsure which parts of your background to emphasize, or if you think your resume would make your case better if it did not follow one of the standard forms outlined either here or in other books on resumes, then you should consider having it professionally written.

Even some professional resume writers have had their resumes written with the help of fellow professionals. They sought the help of someone who could be objective about their background, as well as provide an experienced sounding board to help focus their thoughts.

If You Hire a Pro

The best way to choose a writer is by reputation: the recommendation of a friend, a personnel director, your school placement officer, or someone else knowledgeable in the field.

Some important questions of a potential resume writer:

- "How long have you been writing resumes?"

- "If I'm not satisfied with what you write, will you go over it with me and change it?"

- "Do you charge by the hour or a flat rate?"

There is no sure relation between price and quality, except that you are unlikely to get a good writer for less than $50, even for an uncomplicated resume, and you shouldn't have to pay more than $300 unless your experience is very extensive or complicated. There will be additional charges for printing, and you should discuss up front what any possible charges might be. No matter how much you pay, never assume that the resume you receive is acceptable without checking it thoroughly. It is your career at stake if there are mistakes on your resume!

Few resume services will give you a firm price over the phone, simply because some resumes are too complicated and take too long to do for a predetermined price. Some services will quote you a price that applies to almost all of their customers. Once you decide to use a specific writer, you should insist on a firm price quote before engaging their services. Also, find out how expensive minor changes will be.

COVER LETTERS: QUICK, CLEAR, AND CONCISE

You should always mail a cover letter with your resume. In a cover letter you can show an interest in the company that you can't show in a resume. You can also point out one or two of your skills or accomplishments the company can put to good use. A few relevant and impressive points in a well-written cover letter can draw the interest of the people who will be doing the hiring and cause them to read your resume with more interest and attention.

Make It Personal

The more personal you can get in a cover letter, the better, so long as you keep it professional. If someone known to the person you are writing has recommended that you contact the company, get permission to include his or her name in the letter. If you can get the name of a specific person to send the letter to (instead of "Human Resources Department," for example), address it directly to that person. Unless you are absolutely sure of your information, though, call the company first to verify the spelling of the person's name, correct title, and mailing address. Be sure to put the person's name and title on both the letter and the envelope. This will ensure that your letter will get through to the proper person, even if a new person now occupies this position. It will not always be possible to get the name of a person, but you should always strive to get at least the title of the appropriate hiring manager.

In your letter, be sure to mention something about why you have an interest in the company—so many candidates apply for jobs with no apparent knowledge of what the company does. This conveys the message that they just want any job and might not be a specific fit for this company and position.

To ensure the personal touch, type cover letters in full and print them out individually. Don't try the cheap and easy ways, like using a computer mail merge program or photocopying the body of your letter and typing in the inside address and salutation. You will give the impression that you are mailing to a host of companies and have no particular interest in any one.

You should print your cover letter on the same color and same high-quality paper as your resume. The earlier section of this chapter titled "Getting It on Paper" has tips that apply to both resumes and cover letters.

Cover Letter Basic Format

Your own cover letter may follow a somewhat different format than the following, but to be effective it should definitely include all of the elements mentioned here.

Paragraph 1: State what the position is that you are seeking. It is not always necessary to state how you found out about the position—often you will apply without knowing that a position is open.

Paragraph 2: Include what you know about the company and why you are interested in working there. Mention any prior contact with the company or someone known to the hiring person if relevant. Briefly state your qualifications and what you can offer. (Do not talk about what you cannot do).

Paragraph 3: Close with your phone number and where/when you can be reached. Be sure to make a specific request for an interview, and state when you will follow up by phone (or mail or e-mail if the ad requests no phone calls). Do not wait long—five working days is a reasonable period of time.

One very important point: If you say you're going to follow up, then actually do it! This phone call or e-mail can get your resume noticed when it might otherwise sit in a stack of 225 other resumes. One way to make sure you follow up is to keep a list of the resumes that you've mailed (or e-mailed) that includes the date you sent it *and* the date you told the employer you would contact them further. Make appointments with yourself to follow up with each company on the appropriate dates.

Cover Letter Do's and Don'ts

- *Do* keep your cover letter brief and to the point.

- *Do* be sure it is error-free.

- *Do* accentuate what you can offer the company, not what you hope to gain.

- *Do* be sure your phone number and address are on your cover letter just in case it gets separated from your resume (this does happen).

- *Do* check the watermark by holding the paper up to a light—be sure it is facing forward so it is readable—on the same side as the text, and right-side up.

- *Don't* just repeat information verbatim from your resume.

- *Do* sign your cover letter (or type your name if you are sending it electronically). Blue or black ink are both fine. Do not use red ink.

- *Don't* overuse the personal pronoun "I."

- *Don't* send a generic cover letter—show your personal knowledge of and interest in that particular company.

THANK-YOU LETTERS: ANOTHER WAY TO STAND OUT

Always send a thank-you letter after an interview. So few candidates do this and it is yet another way for you to stand out and make a good impression. Be sure to mention something specific from the interview and restate your interest in the company and the position.

It is generally acceptable to handwrite your thank-you letter on a generic thank-you card (but never a postcard). Make sure handwritten notes are neat and legible. However, if you are in doubt, typing your letter is always the safest bet. If you met with several people, it is fine to send each of them an individual thank-you letter. Call the company if you need to check on the correct spelling of their names. When sending a thank-you letter, remember to:

- Keep it short.

- Proofread it carefully.

- Send it promptly.

After you've impressed an employer with your well-written, error-free cover letter and resume, you certainly don't want to slip up at the finish with a sloppy thank-you letter. Every piece of written material that you send to a potential employer plays a role in getting them to form a positive first—and second and third—impression of you that will lead to that coveted job offer.

CHAPTER THIRTY-FOUR

LAUNCHING A SUCCESSFUL JOB SEARCH

HAVING AN EFFECTIVE RESUME —backed up by well-written cover letters and thank-you notes—is just one element necessary for successfully discovering and obtaining the right position for you. In this chapter, we will discuss some of the other steps and procedures that go into a successful job search.

The first sections of the chapter explain the fundamentals that every jobseeker should know, especially first-time jobseekers. Topics include career planning, finding open positions, contacting employers, and performing well at job interviews. The concluding sections deal with special situations faced by specific types of jobseekers: those who are currently employed, those who have recently lost a job, and college students.

THE BASICS: BEGINNING A JOB SEARCH

If you are new to the job market (as an imminent or recent college graduate or as a person returning to the workforce after a number of years), then you will certainly need to become familiar with all the elements of job seeking presented.

here. Even if you are in the middle of your career and have already held a number of positions, you should find some ideas and tips here that could help with your search for a new job.

Career Planning

The first step to finding your ideal job is to clearly define your objectives. This is better known as career planning (or life planning, if you wish to emphasize the importance of combining a successful career with a happy life). Career planning has become a field of study in and of itself.

If you are thinking of choosing or switching careers, you should keep two things particularly in mind. First, choose a career where you will enjoy most of the day-to-day tasks. This sounds obvious, but most of us have at some point found the idea of a glamour industry or prestigious job title attractive without thinking of the key consideration: Would we enjoy performing the everyday tasks the position entails?

The second key consideration is that you are not merely choosing a career, but also a lifestyle. Career counselors indicate that one of the most common problems people encounter in job seeking is that they fail to consider how well suited they are for a particular position or career. For example, some people, attracted to management consulting by good salaries, early responsibility, and high-level corporate exposure, do not adapt well to the long hours, heavy travel demands, and constant pressure to produce. Be sure to ask yourself how you might adapt to the day-to-day duties and working environment that a specific position requires. Then ask yourself how you might adapt to the demands of that career or industry as a whole.

Choosing Your Strategy

Assuming that you've established your career objectives, the next step of the job search is to develop a strategy. If you don't take the time to develop a plan, you may find yourself going in circles after several weeks of randomly searching for opportunities that always seem just beyond your reach.

The most common job-seeking techniques are:

- Following up on help-wanted advertisements (in the newspaper or online)

- Using employment services

- Relying on personal contacts

- Contacting employers directly (the Direct Contact method)

Each of these approaches can lead to good jobs. However, the Direct Contact method boasts twice the success rate of the others. So unless you have specific reasons to employ other strategies, Direct Contact should form the foundation of your job search. For a complete job campaign, you may choose to use other methods as well, but try to expend at least half your energy on Direct Contact.

Setting Your Schedule

Now that you've targeted a strategy, it's time to work out the details of your job search. The most important detail is setting up a schedule. Of course, since job searches aren't something most people do regularly, it may be hard to estimate how long each step will take. Nonetheless, it is important to have a plan so that you can monitor your progress.

When outlining your job search schedule, have a realistic time frame in mind. If you will be job searching full-time, your search could take at least two months or more. If you can only devote part-time effort, it will probably take at least four months.

You probably know a few people who seem to spend their whole lives searching for a better job in their spare time. Don't be one of them. If you are presently working and don't feel like devoting a lot of energy to job seeking right now, then wait. Focus on enjoying your present position, performing your best on the job, and storing up energy for when you are really ready to begin your job search.

If you are currently unemployed, you should remember that job-hunting is tough work, both physically and emotionally. It is also intellectually demanding work that requires you to be at your best. So don't tire yourself out by working on your job campaign around the clock. At the same time, be sure to discipline yourself. The most logical way to manage your time while looking for a job is to keep your regular working hours.

If you are searching full-time and have decided to choose several different strategies, a good plan is to divide each week and designate some time for each method. By trying several approaches at once, you can evaluate how promising each seems and alter your schedule accordingly. Keep in mind that the majority of openings are filled without being advertised. Remember also that positions advertised on the Internet are just as likely to already be filled as those found in the newspaper!

If you are searching part-time and decide to try several different contact methods, it is best to try them sequentially. You simply won't have enough time to put a meaningful amount of effort into more than one method at once. Estimate the length of your job search, and then allocate so many weeks or months for each contact method, beginning with Direct Contact. The purpose of setting this schedule is not to rush you to your goal but to help you periodically evaluate your progress.

DIRECT CONTACT: THE MOST EFFECTIVE METHOD

Once you have scheduled your time, you are ready to begin your search in earnest. Beginning with the Direct Contact method, the first step is to develop a checklist for categorizing the types of firms for which you'd like to work. You might categorize firms by product line, size, customer type (such as industrial or consumer), growth prospects, or geographical location. Separate your prospect list into three groups. The first 25 percent will be your primary target group, the next 25 percent will be your secondary group, and the remaining names will be your reserve group.

Doing Your Research

You should next determine whether you would be happy working at the firms you are researching and to get a better idea of what their employment needs might be. You also need to obtain enough information to sound highly informed about the company during phone conversations and in mail correspondence. But don't go all out on your research yet; you probably won't be able to arrange interviews with some of these firms, so save your big research effort until you start to arrange interviews. Nevertheless, you should plan to spend several hours researching each firm. Do your research in batches to save time and energy. You should first find out what you can about each of the firms in your primary target group. For answers to specific questions, contact any pertinent professional associations that may be able to help you learn more about an employer. Read industry publications, looking for articles on the firm. Then look up the company on the Internet or try additional resources at your local library. Keep organized, and maintain a folder on each firm.

Here's some information to look for:

- Company size

- President, CEO, or owner's name

- When the company was established

- What the company (and each of its divisions) does

- Benefits that are important to you

An abundance of company information can now be found electronically, through the World Wide Web or commercial online services. Researching companies online is a convenient means of obtaining information quickly and easily. You may search a particular company's Website for current information that may be otherwise unavailable in print. In fact, many companies that maintain a site update their information daily. In addition, you may also search articles written about the company online. Today, most of the nation's largest newspapers, magazines, trade publications, and regional business periodicals have online versions of their publications. To find additional resources, use a search engine like Yahoo! or Google and type in the company's name.

If you discover something that really disturbs you about the firm (they are about to close their only local office), or if you discover that your chances of getting a job there are practically nil (they have just instituted a hiring freeze), then cross them off your prospect list. If possible, supplement your research efforts by contacting individuals who know the firm well. Ideally, you should make an informal contact with someone at that particular firm, but often a direct competitor or a major customer will be able to supply you with just as much information. At the very least, try to obtain whatever printed information the company has available—not just annual reports, but product brochures, company profiles, or catalogs. This information is often available on the Internet.

Getting the Interview

Now it is time to make Direct Contact with the goal of arranging interviews. If you have read any books on job searching, you may have noticed that most of these books tell you to avoid the human resources office like the plague. It is said that the human resources office never hires people; they screen candidates. Unfortunately, this is often the case. If you can identify the appropriate manager with the authority to hire you, you should try to contact that person directly.

The obvious means of initiating Direct Contact are:

- Mail (postal or electronic) • Phone calls

Mail contact is a good choice if you have not been in the job market for a while. You can take your time to prepare a letter, say exactly what you want, and of course include your resume. Remember that employers receive many resumes every day. Don't be surprised if you do not get a response to your inquiry, and don't spend weeks waiting for responses that may never come. If you do send a letter, follow it up (or precede it) with a phone call. This will increase your impact, and because of the initial research you did, it will underscore both your familiarity with and your interest in the firm. Bear in mind that your goal is to make your name a familiar one with prospective employers, so that when a position becomes available, your resume will be one of the first the hiring manager seeks out.

If you send a fax, always follow with a hard copy of your resume and cover letter in the mail. Often, through no fault of your own, a fax will come through illegibly and employers do not often have time to let candidates know.

Cover Calls

Another alternative is to make a "cover call." Your cover call should be just like your cover letter: concise. Your first statement should interest the employer in you. Then try to subtly mention your familiarity with the firm. Don't be overbearing; keep your introduction to three sentences or less. Be pleasant, self-confident, and relaxed. This will greatly increase the chances of the person at the other end of the line developing the conversation. But don't press. If you are asked to follow up with "something in the mail," this signals the conversation's natural end. Don't try to prolong the conversation once it has ended, and don't ask what they want to receive in the mail. Always send your resume and a highly personalized follow-up letter, reminding the addressee of the phone conversation. Always include a cover letter if you are asked to send a resume, and treat your resume and cover letter as a total package. Gear your letter toward the specific position you are applying for and prove why you would be a "good match" for the position.

Unless you are in telephone sales, making smooth and relaxed cover calls will probably not come easily. Practice them on your own and then with your friends or relatives.

If you obtain an interview as a result of a telephone conversation, be sure to send a thank-you note reiterating the points you made during the conversation. You will appear more professional and increase your impact. However, unless specifically requested, don't mail your resume once an interview has been arranged. Take it with you to the interview instead.

You should never show up to seek a professional position without an appointment. Even if you are somehow lucky enough to obtain an interview, you will appear so unprofessional that you will not be seriously considered.

INTERVIEWING: BE PREPARED

As each interview is arranged, begin your in-depth research. You should arrive at an interview knowing the company upside-down and inside out. You need to know the company's products, types of customers, subsidiaries, parent company, principal locations, rank in the industry, sales and profit trends, type of ownership, size, current plans, and much more. By this time you have probably narrowed your job search to one industry. Even if you haven't, you should still be familiar with common industry terms, the trends in the firm's industry, the firm's principal competitors and their relative performance, and the direction in which the industry leaders are headed.

Dig into every resource you can! Surf the Internet. Read the company literature, the trade press, the business press, and if the company is public, call your stockbroker (if you have one) and ask for additional information. If possible, speak to someone at the firm before the interview or, if not, speak to someone at a competing firm. The more time you spend, the better. Even if you feel extremely pressed for time, you should set aside several hours for pre-interview research.

Learn to Relax

If you have been out of the job market for some time, don't be surprised if you find yourself tense during your first few interviews. It will probably happen every time you re-enter the market, not just when you seek your first job after getting out of school.

Tension is natural during an interview, but knowing you have done a thorough research job should put you more at ease. Make a list of questions that you think might be asked in each interview. Think out your answers carefully and practice them with a friend. Tape-record your responses to the problem questions. If you feel particularly unsure of your interviewing skills, arrange your first interviews at firms you are not as interested in. (But remember it is common courtesy to seem enthusiastic about the possibility of working for any firm at which you interview.) Practice again on your own after these first few interviews. Go over the difficult questions that you were asked.

Take some time to really think about how you will convey your work history. Present "bad experiences" as "learning experiences." Instead of saying, "I hated my position as a salesperson because I had to bother people on the phone," say, "I realized that cold-calling was not my strong suit. Though I love working with people, I decided my talents would be best used in a more face-to-face atmosphere." Always find some sort of lesson from previous jobs, as they all have one.

Interview Attire

How important is the proper dress for a job interview? Buying a complete wardrobe, donning new shoes, and having your hair styled every morning are not enough to guarantee you a career position as an investment banker. But on the other hand, if you can't find a clean, conservative suit or won't take the time to wash your hair, then you are just wasting your time by interviewing at all.

Personal grooming is as important as finding appropriate clothes for a job interview. Careful grooming indicates both a sense of thoroughness and self-confidence. This is not the time to make a statement—take out the extra earrings and avoid any garish hair colors not found in nature. Women should not wear excessive makeup, and both men and women should refrain from wearing any perfume or cologne (it only takes a small spritz to leave an allergic interviewer with a fit of sneezing and a bad impression of your meeting). Men should be freshly shaven, even if the interview is late in the day, and men with long hair should have it pulled back and neat.

Men applying for any professional position should wear a suit, preferably in a conservative color such as navy or charcoal gray. It is easy to get away with wearing the same dark suit to more than one interview at the same company; just be sure to wear a different shirt and tie each day you are interviewed there.

Women seeking professional positions should also wear a business suit. This is usually true even at companies where pants are acceptable attire for female employees. As much as you may disagree with this guideline, the more prudent time to fight this standard is after you land the job.

The final selection of candidates for a job opening won't be determined by dress, of course. However, inappropriate dress can quickly eliminate a first-round candidate. So while you shouldn't spend a fortune on a new wardrobe, you should be sure that your clothes are adequate. The key is to dress at least as formally or slightly more formally and more conservatively than the position would suggest.

What to Bring

Be complete. Everyone needs a watch, a pen, and a notepad. Finally, a briefcase or a leather-bound folder (containing extra, unfolded, copies of your resume) will help complete the look of professionalism.

Sometimes the interviewer will be running behind schedule. Don't be upset; be sympathetic. There is often pressure to interview a lot of candidates and to quickly fill a demanding position. So be sure to come to your interview with good reading material to keep yourself occupied and relaxed.

The First Interview

The very beginning of a first interview is the most important part because it determines the tone for the rest of it. Those first few moments are especially crucial. Do you smile when you meet? Do you establish enough eye contact, but not too much? Do you walk into the office with a self-assured and confident stride? Do you shake hands firmly? Do you make small talk easily without being garrulous? It is human nature to judge people by that first impression, so make sure it is a good one. But most of all, try to be yourself.

Often the interviewer will begin, after the small talk, by telling you about the company, the division, the department, or perhaps the position. Because of your detailed research, the information about the company should be repetitive for you, and the interviewer would probably like nothing better than to avoid this regurgitation of the company biography. So if you can do so tactfully, indicate to the interviewer that you are very familiar with the firm. If he or she seems intent on providing you with background information, despite your hints, then don't object.

But be sure to remain attentive. If you can manage to generate a brief discussion of the company or the industry at this point without being forceful, great. It will help to further build rapport, underscore your interest, and increase your impact.

Soon (if it didn't begin that way) the interviewer will begin the questions, many of which you will have already practiced. This period of the interview usually falls into one of two categories (or somewhere in between): either a structured interview, where the interviewer has a prescribed set of questions to ask; or an unstructured interview, where the interviewer will ask only leading questions to get you to talk about yourself, your experiences, and your goals. Try to sense as quickly as possible in which direction the interviewer wishes to proceed. This will make the interviewer feel more relaxed and in control of the situation.

Remember to keep attuned to the interviewer and make the length of your answers appropriate to the situation. If you are really unsure as to how detailed a response the interviewer is seeking, then ask.

As the interview progresses, the interviewer will probably mention some of the most important responsibilities of the position. If applicable, draw parallels between your experience and the demands of the position as detailed by the interviewer. Describe your past experience in the same manner that you do on your resume: emphasizing results and achievements and not merely describing activities. But don't exaggerate. Be on the level about your abilities.

The first interview is often the toughest, where many candidates are screened out. If you are interviewing for a very competitive position, you will have to make an impression that will last. Focus on a few of your greatest strengths that are relevant to the position. Develop these points carefully, state them again in different words, and then try to summarize them briefly at the end of the interview.

Often the interviewer will pause toward the end and ask if you have any questions. Particularly in a structured interview, this might be the one chance to really show your knowledge of and interest in the firm. Have a list prepared of specific questions that are of real interest to you. Let your questions subtly show your research and your knowledge of the firm's activities. It is wise to have an extensive list of questions ready, because several of your questions may already be answered during the interview.

Make sure that you don't turn your opportunity to ask questions into an interrogation. You should avoid reading directly from your list of questions, and ask questions that you are fairly certain the interviewer can answer (remember how you feel when you cannot answer a question during an interview).

Even if you are unable to determine the salary range beforehand, do not ask about it during the first interview. You can always ask later. Above all, don't ask about fringe benefits until you have been offered a position. (Then be sure to get all the details.)

A few more interview tips:

- Try not to be negative about anything during the interview, particularly any past employer or any previous job.

- Be cheerful. Everyone likes to work with someone who seems to be happy.

- Even if you detest your current/former job or manager, do not make disparaging comments. The interviewer may construe this as a sign of a potential attitude problem and not consider you a strong candidate.

- Don't let a tough question throw you off base. If you don't know the answer to a question, simply say so—do not apologize. Just smile. Nobody can answer every question—particularly some of the questions that are asked in job interviews.

Further Interviews

Before your first interview, you may be able to determine how many rounds of interviews there usually are for positions at your level. (Of course it may differ quite a bit even within the different levels of one firm.) Usually you can count on attending at least two or three interviews, although some firms are known to give a minimum of six interviews for all professional positions. While you should be more relaxed as you return for subsequent interviews, the pressure will be on. The more prepared you are, the better.

Depending on what information you are able to obtain, you might want to vary your strategy quite a bit from interview to interview. For instance, if the first interview is a screening interview, then be sure a few of your strengths really stand out. On the other hand, if later interviews are primarily with people who are in a position to veto your hiring, but not to push it forward, then you should primarily focus on building rapport as opposed to reiterating and developing your key strengths.

If it looks as though your skills and background do not match the position the interviewer was hoping to fill, ask him or her if there is another division or subsidiary that perhaps could profit from your talents.

After the Interview

Write a follow-up letter immediately after the interview, while it is still fresh in the interviewer's mind. Not only is this a thank-you, but it also gives you the chance to provide the interviewer with any details you may have forgotten (as long as they can be tactfully added in). If you haven't heard from the interviewer within a week of sending your thank-you letter, call to stress your continued interest in the firm and the position. If you lost any points during the interview for any reason, this letter can help you regain your footing. Be polite and make sure to stress your continued interest and competency to fill the position. Just don't forget to proofread it thoroughly. If you are unsure of the spelling of the interviewer's name, call the receptionist and ask.

THE BALANCING ACT: LOOKING FOR A JOB WHILE CURRENTLY EMPLOYED

If you are currently employed, job searching will be particularly tiring because it must be done in addition to your normal work responsibilities. So don't overwork yourself to the point where you show up to interviews looking exhausted or start to slip behind at your current job. On the other hand, don't be tempted to quit your present job. The extra hours are worth it. Searching for a job while you have one puts you in a position of strength.

Making Contact

If you must be at your office during the business day, then you have additional problems to deal with. How can you work interviews into the business day? And if you work in an open office, how can you even call to set up interviews? Obviously, you should keep up the effort and the appearances on your present job. So maximize your use of the lunch hour, early mornings, and late afternoons for calling. If you keep trying, you'll be surprised how often you will be able to reach the executive you are trying to contact during your out-of-office hours. You can often catch people as early as 8 A.M. and as late as 6 P.M.

Scheduling Interviews

Your inability to interview at any time other than lunch just might work to your advantage. If you can, try to set up as many interviews as possible for your lunch hour. This will go a long way to creating a relaxed atmosphere. But be sure the interviews don't stray too far from the agenda on hand.

Lunchtime interviews are much easier to obtain if you have substantial career experience. People with less experience will often find no alternative to taking time off for interviews. If you have to take time off, you have to take time off. But try to do this as little as possible. Try to take the whole day off in order to avoid being blatantly obvious about your job search, and try to schedule two to three interviews for the same day. (It is very difficult to maintain an optimum level of energy at more than three interviews in one day.) You should explain to the interviewer why you might have to juggle your interview schedule. He or she should honor the respect you're showing your current employer by minimizing your days off, and it may be to your advantage to indicate that other companies are also interested in you.

References

What do you tell an interviewer who asks for references from your current employer? Just say that while you are happy to have your former employers contacted, you are trying to keep your job search confidential and would rather that your current employer not be contacted until you have been given a firm offer.

WHEN YOU'RE FIRED OR LAID OFF:
PICKING YOURSELF BACK UP

If you've been fired or laid off, just remember that you are not the first and will not be the last to go through this traumatic experience. In today's changing economy, thousands of people lose their jobs every year. Even if you were terminated with just cause, do not lose heart. Remember, being fired is not a reflection on you as a person. It is usually a reflection of your company's staffing needs and its perception of your recent job performance and attitude. And if you were not performing up to par or enjoying your work, then you will probably be better off at another company anyway.

A thorough job search could take months, so be sure to negotiate a reasonable severance package, if possible, and determine to what benefits, such as health insurance, you are still legally entitled. Also, register for unemployment compensation immediately.

Although you are probably feeling a real sense of urgency, you still shouldn't start your job search with a flurry of unplanned activity. Start by choosing a strategy and working out a plan. Now is not the time for major changes in your life. If possible, remain in the same career and in the same geographical location, at least until you have been working again for a while. On the other hand, if the only industry for which you are trained is leaving or is severely depressed in your area, then you should give prompt consideration to moving or switching careers.

Avoid mentioning you were fired when arranging interviews, but be prepared for the question "Why were you fired?" during an interview. If you were laid off as a result of downsizing, briefly explain, being sure to reinforce that your job loss was not due to performance. If you were in fact fired, be honest, but try to detail the reason as favorably as possible and portray what you have learned from your mistakes. If you are confident one of your past managers will give you a good reference, tell the interviewer to contact that person. Do not speak negatively of your past employer and try not to sound particularly worried about your status of being temporarily unemployed.

Finally, don't spend too much time reflecting on why you were let go or how you might have avoided it. Think positively, look to the future, and be sure to follow a careful plan during your job search.

THE COLLEGE STUDENT: CONDUCTING YOUR FIRST JOB SEARCH

While college students will be able to apply many of the basics covered earlier in this chapter to their job search, there are some elements unique to their situation.

Perhaps the biggest problem college students face is lack of experience. Many schools have internship programs designed to give students exposure to the field of their choice, as well as the opportunity to make valuable contacts. Check out your school's career services department to see what internships are available. If your school does not have a formal internship program or if there are no available internships that appeal to you, try contacting local businesses and offering your services. Often, businesses will be more than willing to have an extra pair of hands (especially if those hands are unpaid!) for a day or two each week. Or try contacting school alumni to see if you can "shadow" them for a few days and see what their daily duties are like.

Informational Interviews

Although many jobseekers do not do this, it can be extremely helpful to arrange an informational interview with a college alumnus or someone else who works in your desired industry. You interview them about their job, their company, and their industry with questions you have prepared in advance. This can be done over the phone but is usually done in person. This will provide you with a contact in the industry who may give you more valuable information—or perhaps even a job opportunity—in the future. Always follow up with a thank-you letter that includes your contact information. The goal is to try to begin building experience and establishing contacts as early as possible in your college career.

What do you do if, for whatever reason, you weren't able to get experience directly related to your desired career? First, look at your previous jobs and see if there's anything you can highlight. Did you supervise or train other employees? Did you reorganize the accounting system or boost productivity in some way? Accomplishments like these demonstrate leadership, responsibility, and innovation—qualities that most companies look for in employees. And don't forget volunteer activities and school clubs, which can also showcase these traits.

On-Campus Recruiting

Companies often send recruiters to interview on-site at various colleges. This gives students a chance to interview with companies that may not have interviewed them otherwise. This is particularly true if a company schedules "open" interviews, in which the only screening process is who is first in line at the sign-ups. Of course, since many more applicants gain interviews in this format, this also means that many more people are rejected. The on-campus interview is generally a screening interview, to see if it is worth the company's time to invite you in for a second interview. So do everything possible to make yourself stand out from the crowd.

The first step, of course, is to check out any and all information your school's career center has on the company. If the information seems out of date, check out the company on the Internet or call the company's headquarters and ask for any printed information.

Many companies will host an informational meeting for interviewees, often the evening before interviews are scheduled to take place. *Do not miss this meeting.* The recruiter will almost certainly ask if you attended. Make an effort to stay after the meeting and talk with the company's representatives. Not only does this give you an opportunity to find out more information about both the company and the position, it also makes you stand out in the recruiter's mind. If there's a particular company that you had your heart set on, but you weren't able to get an interview with them, attend the information session anyway. You may be able to persuade the recruiter to squeeze you into the schedule. (Or you may discover that the company really isn't the right fit for you after all.)

Try to check out the interview site beforehand. Some colleges may conduct "mock" interviews that take place in one of the standard interview rooms. Or you may be able to convince a career counselor (or even a custodian) to let you sneak a peek during off-hours. Either way, having an idea of the room's setup will help you to mentally prepare.

You should try to arrive at least fifteen minutes early to the interview. The recruiter may be ahead of schedule and might meet you early. But don't be surprised if previous interviews have run over, resulting in your thirty-minute slot being reduced to twenty minutes (or less). Don't complain or appear anxious; just use the time you do have as efficiently as possible to showcase the reasons you are the ideal candidate. Staying calm and composed in these situations will work to your advantage.

SOME LAST WORDS: KEEP ON TRYING

Even if you have an excellent resume—full of effective buzz words—and a well-prepared job-seeking campaign, looking for a job can be really tough. Again and again during your job search you will face rejection. You will be rejected when you apply for interviews. You will be rejected after interviews. For every job offer you finally receive, you probably will have been rejected many times. Don't let rejections slow you down. Keep reminding yourself that the sooner you go out, start your job search, and get those rejections flowing in, the closer you will be to obtaining the job you want.